Chopin
2010

WYDANIE NARODOWE
DZIEŁ FRYDERYKA CHOPINA

NATIONAL EDITION
OF THE WORKS OF FRYDERYK CHOPIN

PRELUDES
Opp. 28, 45

NATIONAL EDITION
Edited by JAN EKIER

Foundation
for the National Edition
of the Works of Fryderyk Chopin

PWM
EDITION

SERIES A. WORKS PUBLISHED DURING CHOPIN'S LIFETIME. VOLUME VII

FRYDERYK CHOPIN

PRELUDIA
Op. 28, 45

WYDANIE NARODOWE
Redaktor naczelny: JAN EKIER

FUNDACJA WYDANIA NARODOWEGO
POLSKIE WYDAWNICTWO MUZYCZNE SA
WARSZAWA 2024

SERIA A. UTWORY WYDANE ZA ŻYCIA CHOPINA. TOM VII

Redakcja tomu: Jan Ekier, Paweł Kamiński

Komentarz wykonawczy i *Komentarz źródłowy (skrócony)* dołączone są do nut głównej
serii *Wydania Narodowego* oraz do strony internetowej www.chopin-nationaledition.com

Pełne *Komentarze źródłowe* do poszczególnych tomów wydawane są oddzielnie.

Wydany w oddzielnym tomie *Wstęp do Wydania Narodowego Dzieł Fryderyka Chopina*
– 1. Zagadnienia edytorskie obejmuje całokształt ogólnych problemów wydawniczych,
zaś *Wstęp... – 2. Zagadnienia wykonawcze* – całokształt ogólnych problemów interpretacyjnych.
Pierwsza część *Wstępu* jest także dostępna na stronie www.pwm.com.pl

Editors of this Volume: Jan Ekier, Paweł Kamiński

A *Performance Commentary* and a *Source Commentary (abridged)* are included in the
music of the main series of the *National Edition* and available on www.chopin-nationaledition.com

Full *Source Commentaries* on each volume are published separately.

The *Introduction to the National Edition of the Works of Fryderyk Chopin*,
1. Editorial Problems, published as a separate volume, covers general matters concerning the publication.
The *Introduction... 2. Problems of Performance* covers all general questions of the interpretation.
First part of the *Introduction* is also available on the website www.pwm.com.pl

Preludia op. 28 / Preludes Op. 28

Nr 1 C-dur / No. 1 C major — page / s. 13

Nr 2 a-moll / No. 2 A minor — page / s. 14

Nr 3 G-dur / No. 3 G major — page / s. 15

Nr 4 e-moll / No. 4 E minor — page / s. 17

Nr 5 D-dur / No. 5 D major — page / s. 18

Nr 6 h-moll / No. 6 B minor — page / s. 19

Nr 7 A-dur / No. 7 A major — page / s. 21

Nr 8 fis-moll / No. 8 F♯ minor — page / s. 21

Nr 9 E-dur / No. 9 E major — page / s. 25

Nr 10 cis-moll / No. 10 C♯ minor — page / s. 26

Nr 11 H-dur / No. 11 B major — page / s. 27

Nr 12 gis-moll / No. 12 G♯ minor — page / s. 28

Nr 13 Fis-dur / No. 13 F♯ major — page / s. 31

Nr 14 es-moll / No. 14 E♭ minor — page / s. 33

Nr 15 Des-dur / No. 15 D♭ major — page / s. 34

Nr 16 b-moll / No. 16 B♭ minor — page / s. 38

Nr 17 As-dur / No. 17 A♭ major — page / s. 42

Nr 18 f-moll / No. 18 F minor — page / s. 46

Nr 19 Es-dur / No. 19 E♭ major — page / s. 48

Nr 20 c-moll / No. 20 C minor — page / s. 51

Nr 21 B-dur / No. 21 B♭ major — page / s. 52

Nr 22 g-moll / No. 22 G minor — page / s. 54

Nr 23 F-dur / No. 23 F major — page / s. 56

Nr 24 d-moll / No. 24 D minor — page / s. 57

Preludium cis-moll op. 45 / Prelude in C♯ minor Op. 45

page / s. 62

o Preludiach...

op. 28

„Dostaniesz Preludia wkrótce."

15 XI 1838

„[...] ani ci mogę manuskryptu posłać, bom nie skończył. Chorowałem przez te ostatnie dwa tygodnie jak pies [...]. To jednak ma wpływ na Preludia, które Pan Bóg wie kiedy dostaniesz."

3 XII 1838

„Tymczasem moje manuskrypta śpią, a ja spać nie mogę, tylko kaszlę, i od dawna plastrami obłożony, czekam wiosny albo czego innego... Jutro jadę do owego przecudnego klasztoru V a l d e m o s a pisać w celi starego mnicha [...]. Myślę ci moje Preludia [...] wkrótce posłać."

14 XII 1838

„Nie mogę Preludiów ci posłać, bo nieskończone; lepiej się mam i pospieszę, [...]"

28 XII 1838

„Posyłam ci Preludie. P r z e p i s z , t y i W o l f f ; myślę, że błędów nie ma. Dasz p r z e p i s a n e P r o b s t o w i , a m a n u s k r y p t P l e y e l o w i ."

22 I 1839

Z listów F. Chopina do Juliana Fontany w Paryżu, Palma 1838, Valldemosa 1839.

„Przesyłam Panu nareszcie moje Preludia dokończone na Pańskim pianinie, które nadeszło w jak najlepszym stanie – nie zaszkodziło mu ani morze, ani niepogoda, ani urząd celny w Palmie. Poleciłem Fontanie, żeby wręczył Panu mój rękopis."

Z listu F. Chopina do Kamila Pleyela w Paryżu, Valldemosa 22 I 1839.

„Bardzo bym chciał, żeby moje Preludia były dedykowane P l e y e l o w i [...]. Jeżeli P l e y e l nie będzie chciał opuścić Ballady, to Preludia d e d y k u j S c h u m a n n o w i . [...] O zmianie dedykacji powiesz Probstowi, jak się z Pleyelem uradzisz."

Z listu F. Chopina do Juliana Fontany w Paryżu, Marsylia III 1839.

„Pleyel do mnie pisał, żeś bardzo obligeant, żeś poprawił Preludia."

Z listu F. Chopina do Juliana Fontany w Paryżu, Nohant 8 VIII 1839.

op. 28 nr 6

„Jest jedno [Preludium] które mu przyszło do głowy w pewien dżdżysty i ponury wieczór, a które pogrąża duszę
w straszliwym przygnębieniu. [...] Kiedy zwróciłam jego uwagę na odgłos kropel wody, które rzeczywiście miarowo
spadały na dach, powiedział, że ich nie słyszał. Oburzył się nawet, że tłumaczę to jako wyraz harmonii naśladowczej [...].
Kompozycja jego z tego wieczora była w istocie pełna kropel deszczu, odbijających się echem od dźwięcznych
dachówek klasztoru, ale przekładały się one w jego wyobraźni i melodii na łzy spadające z nieba na jego serce."

George Sand, *Histoire de ma vie*, Paryż 1854-55.

op. 28 nr 17

„Pamiętam, że raz, gdy grałem 17. Preludium Chopina, pani Dubois powiedziała, że w końcowym jego odcinku
Chopin miał zwyczaj grać nutę basową [As₁] z dużą siłą (mimo że wszystko pozostałe grał diminuendo).
Ową nutę u d e r z a ł zawsze w ten sam sposób i z j e d n a k o w ą siłą ze względu na znaczenie, jakie jej nadawał.
Akcentował ją i wyodrębniał, ponieważ pomysł tego Preludium opiera się na dźwięku starego zamkowego zegara,
wybijającego j e d e n a s t ą godzinę. [...] Chopin nalegał zawsze na to, aby nuta basowa była uderzana
z t ą s a m ą siłą – bez diminuendo, ponieważ zegar nie może dzwonić diminuendo."

I. J. Paderewski, M. Lawton, *The Paderewski Memoirs*, Londyn 1939.

op. 28 nr 20

„Uwaga d l a w y d a w c y (z ulicy Rochechouart): małe ustępstwo na rzecz pana ***, który często ma rację."

Adnotacja przy powtórzeniu taktów 5-8, zaznaczonym skrótowo w autografie edycyjnym tego *Preludium*.

„[Pod jego palcami] były to akordy rodem raczej z nieba niż z tej ziemi, akordy pełne natchnienia,
które sięgnie wieczności."

Z listu Jane Stirling do Ludwiki Jędrzejewiczowej w Warszawie, Paryż 12 VI 1850.

op. 45

„Wczoraj, we czwartek, stanąłem tutaj. Zrobiłem Preludium cis-moll dla S c h l e s i n g e r a, krótkie, tak jak chciał.
[...] dam mu do owego Albumu ten dzisiejszy Prelud, który dobrze modulowany, mogę śmiało posłać."

„Posyłam ci Preludium większym charakterem dla Schlesingera, a mniejszym dla Mechettego. Obetniesz p o d o b n i e
manuskrypt mojego pisania Poloneza, złożysz (zanumerowawszy karty) podobnie do owego Preludium [...].
Także n i e z a p o m n i j dodać o p u s na Polonezie, a następny n u m e r na Preludium, co poślesz do Wiednia.
Nie wiem jak się pisze Czerniszewowa [...]: czy Tscher, czy Tcher? [...], czy Elisabeth i czy Tschernischef, czy ff,
[dowiedz się] jak mają zwyczaj pisać."

Z listów F. Chopina do Juliana Fontany w Paryżu, Nohant 30 IX i 6 X 1841.

about the Preludes...

Op. 28

"You shall be getting the Preludes soon."

15 November 1838

*"[...] nor can I send you the manuscript, because I have not finished. I was sick like a dog this past fortnight [...].
It does affect the Preludes, which the Lord God knows when you will get."*

3 December 1838

*"Meanwhile my manuscripts are sleeping, and I cannot sleep, all I do is cough, and having been long covered in plasters
await spring or else... Tomorrow I am going to that most wonderful monastery Valdemosa to write in the cell
of an old monk [...] I think I should be sending you my Preludes [...] soon."*

14 December 1838

"I cannot send you the Preludes because they are not finished; I am feeling better and I will hurry [...]"

28 December 1838

*"I am sending you the Preludes. Copy them, you and Wolff; I think there are no mistakes. Give the copy
to Probst and the manuscript to Pleyel."*

22 January 1839

From letters by F. Chopin to Julian Fontana in Paris, Palma 1838, Valldemosa 1839.

*"Dear friend. At last I am sending you my Preludes, completed on your piano which arrived in the best of conditions
– it was not harmed by the sea, nor the bad weather, nor the customs office in Palma. I have instructed Fontana
to give you my manuscript."*

From F. Chopin's letter to Camille Pleyel in Paris, Valldemosa, 22 January 1839.

*"I very much want my Preludes to be dedicated to Pleyel [...]. If Pleyel will not agree to leave out the Ballade,
dedicate the Preludes to Schumann. [...] Tell Probst about the changed dedication after you speak with Pleyel."*

From F. Chopin's letter to Julian Fontana in Paris, Marseilles, March 1839.

"Pleyel wrote to me that you are very obligeant, that you have proof-read the Preludes."

From a letter by F. Chopin to Julian Fontana in Paris, Nohant, 8 August 1839.

Op. 28 no. 6

"There is one [Prelude] which he conceived on a certain damp and gloomy evening and which plunges the spirit
into a terrible despair. [...] When I drew his attention to the sound of droplets of water which really did fall rhythmically
onto the roof, he said he had not heard them. He was even angry that I was interpreting it as an expression of imitative
harmony [...]. His composition from that evening was truly full of raindrops, bouncing with an echo off the monastery's
resonant roof-tiles, but in his imagination and melody they became translated into tears falling from the sky onto his heart".

George Sand, *Histoire de ma vie*, Paris 1854-55.

Op. 28 no. 17

"I remember once when I was playing the 17th Prelude of Chopin, Madame Dubois said that Chopin himself used
to play that bass note [A♭₁] in the final section (in spite of playing everything else diminuendo) with great strength.
He always s t r u c k that note in the same way and with the s a m e strength, because of the meaning he attached to it.
He accentuated that bass note—he proclaimed it, because the idea of that Prelude is based on the sound of an old clock
in the castle which strikes the e l e v e n t h hour. [...] Chopin always insisted the bass note should be struck with the s a m e
strength—no diminuendo, because the clock knows no diminuendo."

I. J. Paderewski, M. Lawton, *The Paderewski Memoirs*, London 1939.

Op. 28 no. 20

"Note f o r t h e p u b l i s h e r (in Rue de Rochechouart): a small concession in favour of Monsieur ***, who is often right."

Note at the repetition of bars 5-8, marked in abbreviated fashion on the manuscript for publication of this *Prelude*.

"Those chords [which came from under his fingers] were celestial rather than of this earth, they were chords
full of an inspiration reaching towards eternity."

From a letter by Jane Stirling to Ludwika Jędrzejewicz in Warsaw, Paris, 12 June 1850.

Op. 45

"Yesterday, Thursday, I stopped here. I did the Prelude in C♯ minor for S c h l e s i n g e r, short, the way he wanted it.
[...] I shall give him for his Album today's Prelude, which being well modulated I can boldly send."

"I am sending you the Prelude in bigger script for Schlesinger and smaller for Mechetti. You shall s i m i l a r l y
cut my manuscript of the Polonaise and fold it (having numbered the pages) after the fashion of the Prelude [...].
Also d o n o t f o r g e t to add the o p u s on the Polonaise and the subsequent number on the Prelude, which you
will be sending to Vienna. I do not know how to spell Czernicheff [...]: Tscher or Tcher? [...], is it Elisabeth
and is it Tschernischef or ff, [find out] what is their manner of spelling it."

From letters by F. Chopin to Julian Fontana in Paris, Nohant, 30 September and 6 October 1841.

24 Préludes

A son ami Camille Pleyel

op. 28 nr 1

* Patrz *Komentarz źródłowy i wykonawczy.*
  Vide Source and *Performance Commentaries.*

FWN 7 **A VII**

16

Allegro molto

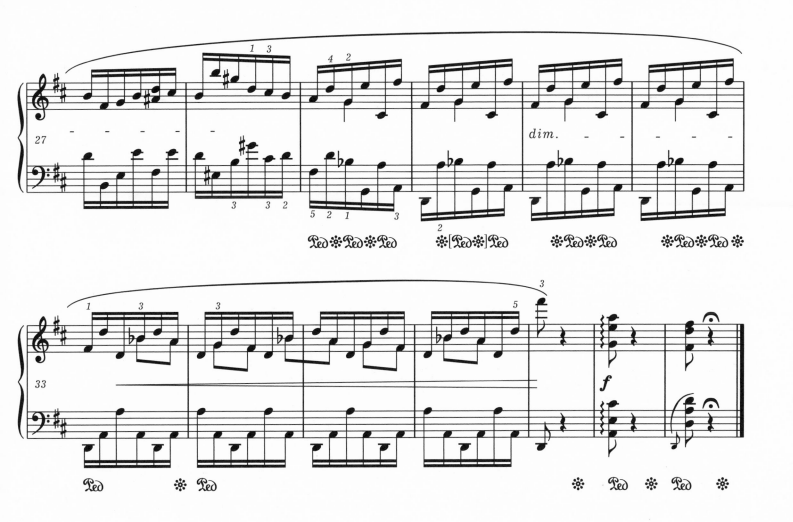

op. 28 nr 6

Lento assai

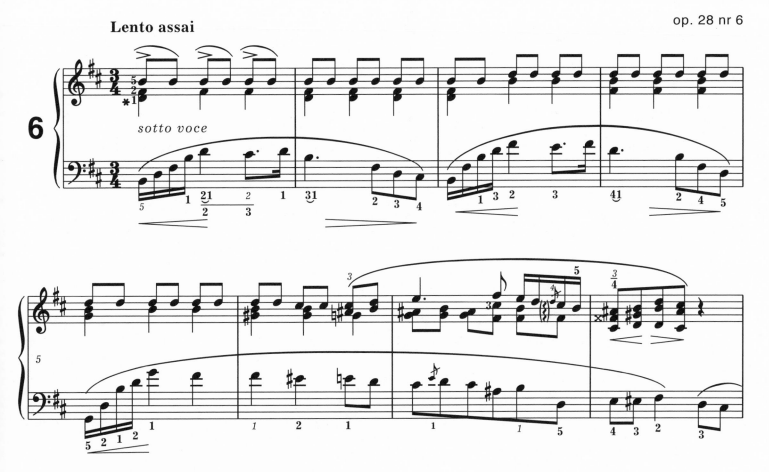

sotto voce

* Palcowanie Chopinowskie tego *Preludium* pochodzi w całości z egzemplarzy lekcyjnych.
Chopin's fingering in this *Prelude* comes entirely from pupils' copies.

* ossia: **pp**

** Kwestia przetrzymania lub powtórzenia nuty *H₁* - patrz *Komentarz źródłowy*.
Question of sustaining or repeating the note *B₁* - *vide Source Commentary*.

20

FWN 7 **A VII**

Andantino
dolce

op. 28 nr 8

Molto agitato

* Patrz *Komentarz wykonawczy.*
  Vide Performance Commentary.

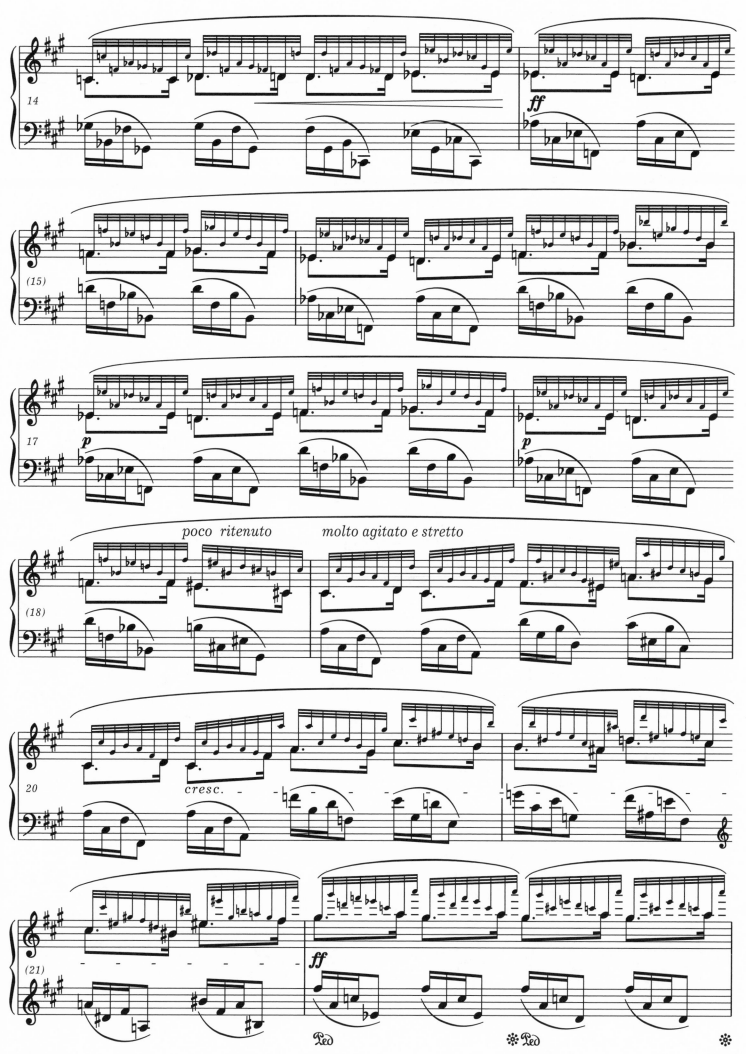

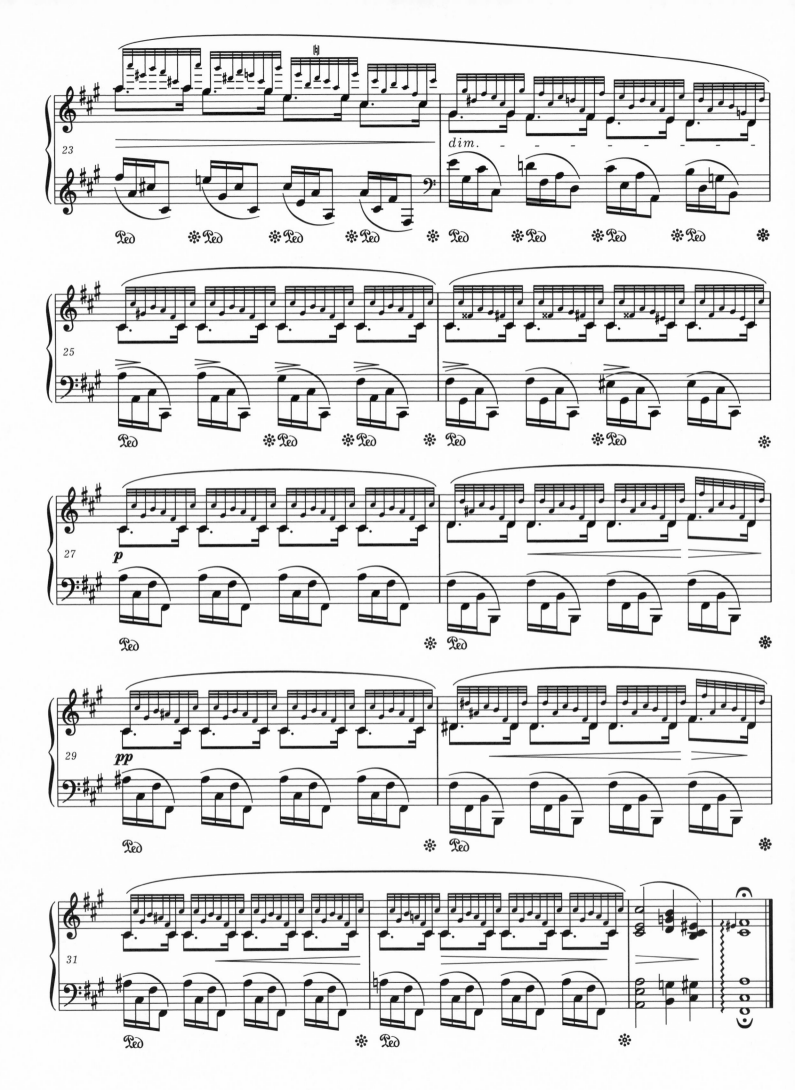

* Wersja oryginalna bez dolnych dźwięków H_2 i E_1 (skala fortepianu Chopina sięgała tylko do C_1). Patrz *Komentarz źródłowy*.
  Without the lower notes B_2 and E_1 in the sources (Chopin's piano only went down to C_1). *Vide Source Commentary*.

25

* Znak w jednym z egzemplarzy lekcyjnych sugeruje przerwanie łuku w tym miejscu.
  A sign in one of the pupils' copies suggests breaking the slur here.

** Patrz *Komentarz wykonawczy.*
  Vide Performance Commentary.

* Inne palcowanie - patrz *Komentarz wykonawczy*.
  For a different fingering *vide Performance Commentary.*

** Dopuszczalny wariant przy założeniu pomyłki Chopina. Patrz *Komentarz źródłowy*.
   A permissible variant supposing Chopin's error. *Vide Source Commentary.*

* Patrz *Komentarz źródłowy.*
Vide Source Commentary.

* Widełki w autografie niejasne. Można je również odczytać jako ———.
The sign is illegible in the autograph, it can also be understood as ———.

Sostenuto

15

* Palcowanie Chopinowskie tego *Preludium* pochodzi w całości z egzemplarzy lekcyjnych.
  Chopin's fingering in this *Prelude* comes entirely from pupils' copies.

Presto con fuoco

* Znak w egzemplarzu lekcyjnym mało czytelny, może również oznaczać **pp**.
  The sign in a pupil's copy is hardly legible. It may also denote **pp**.

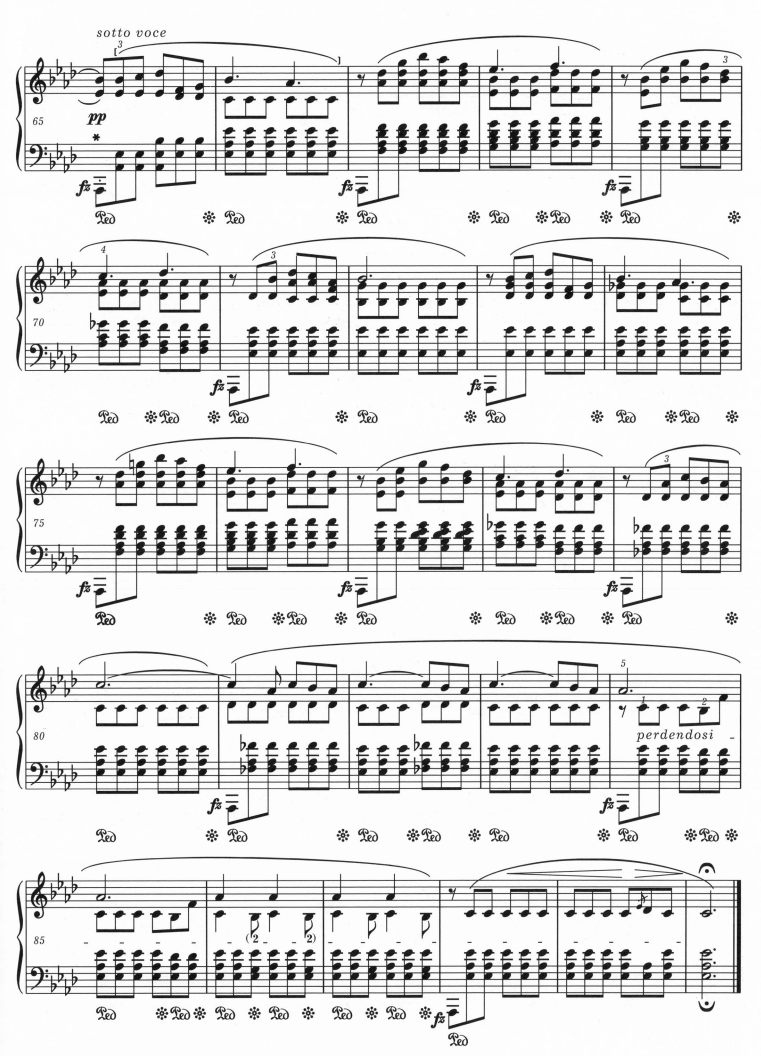

* Wykonanie 11 uderzeń nuty pedałowej *As₁* - patrz *Komentarz wykonawczy* oraz cytaty przed tekstem nutowym.
  For performance of 11 strokes of the pedal point *A♭₁* see quotations on page 11 and the *Performance Commentary.*

45

Allegro molto

* Dopuszczalny wariant przy założeniu pomyłki Chopina. Patrz *Komentarz źródłowy.*
A permissible variant supposing Chopin's error. *Vide Source Commentary.*

50

op. 28 nr 20

* Patrz *Komentarz źródłowy.*
 Vide Source Commentary.

** W jednym z autografów zamiast akcentu jest **ff**.
 In one of the autographs there is **ff** instead of the accent.

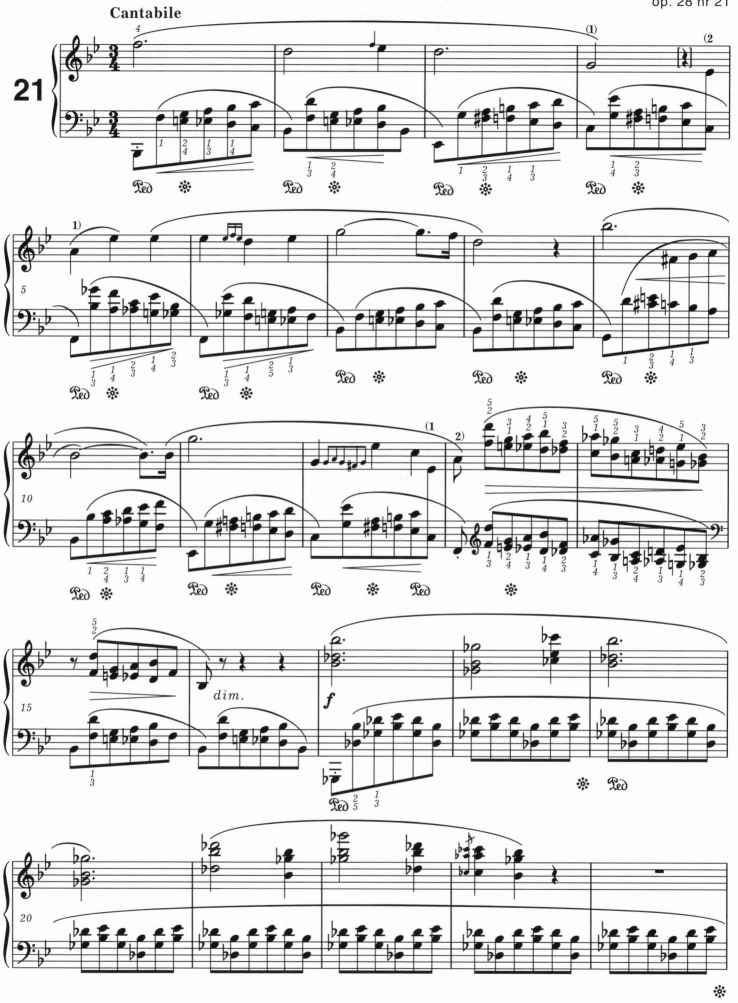

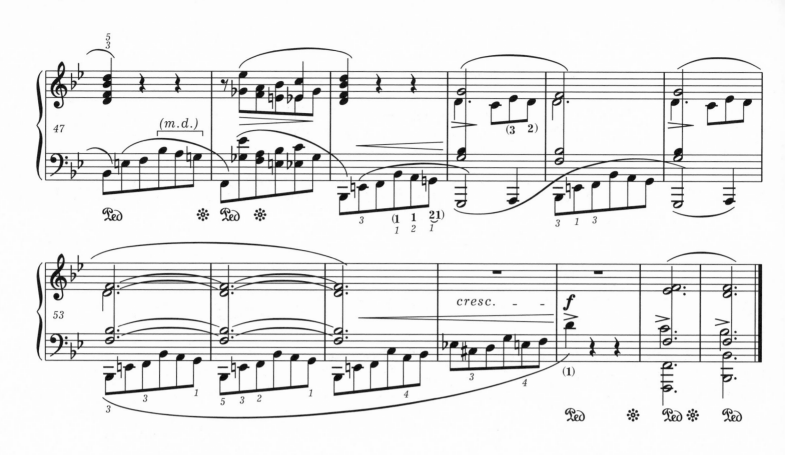

op. 28 nr 22

Molto agitato

* Kwestia łukowania partii lewej ręki - patrz *Komentarz źródłowy i wykonawczy*.
  Slurring of the left hand part is discussed in the *Source* and *Performance Commentaries*.

* Zakładając omyłkowe opuszczenie łuków przez Chopina, można dopuścić następujący wariant:
  Supposing Chopin omitted the ties by mistake, the following variant may be permissible:

Moderato
delicatissimo

23

poco ritenuto   in tempo

op. 28 nr 24

Allegro appassionato

60

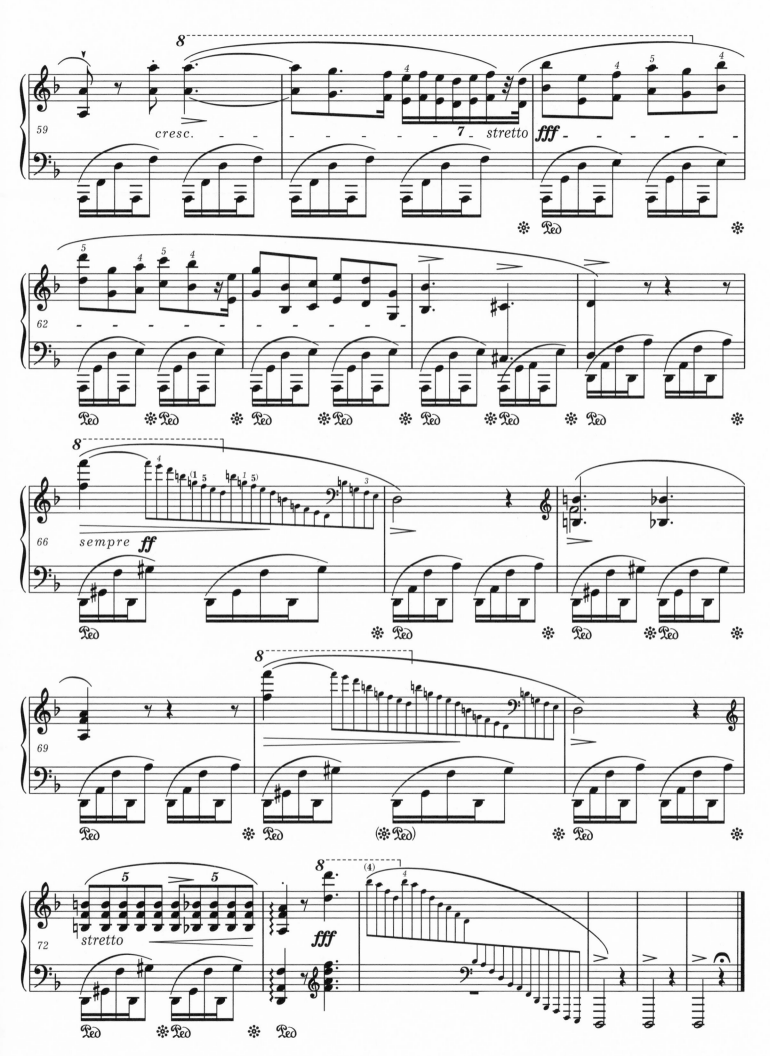

Prélude

A Mademoiselle la Princesse Elisabeth Czernicheff

op. 45

* Pedalizacja - patrz *Komentarz wykonawczy i źródłowy.*
For pedalling *vide Performance* and *Source Commentaries.*

* W jednym ze źródeł **f** znajduje się dopiero na początku t. 32.
  In one of the sources **f** is only found at the beginning of bar 32.

Cadenza
a piacere

leggierissimo

dimin.

Okładka i opracowanie graficzne · Cover design and graphics: MARIA EKIER
Tłumaczenie angielskie · English translation: ELŻBIETA KRAJEWSKA

Fundacja Wydania Narodowego Dzieł Fryderyka Chopina
ul. Okólnik 2, pok. 405, 00-368 Warszawa
www.chopin-nationaledition.com

Polskie Wydawnictwo Muzyczne SA
al. Krasińskiego 11a, 31-111 Kraków
www.pwm.com.pl

Wyd. IV poprawione. Printed in Poland 2024. Drukarnia REGIS Sp. z o.o.
ul. Napoleona 4, 05-230 Kobyłka

ISBN 83-87202-38-X

WYDANIE NARODOWE DZIEŁ FRYDERYKA CHOPINA

Plan edycji

Seria A. UTWORY WYDANE ZA ŻYCIA CHOPINA

Seria B. UTWORY WYDANE POŚMIERTNIE

(Tytuły w nawiasach kwadratowych [] są tytułami zrekonstruowanymi przez WN, tytuły w nawiasach prostych // są dotychczas używanymi, z pewnością lub dużym prawdopodobieństwem, nieautentycznymi tytułami)

1 **A I**   **Ballady** op. 23, 38, 47, 52

2 **A II**   **Etiudy** op. 10, 25, Trzy Etiudy (Méthode des Méthodes)

3 **A III**   **Impromptus** op. 29, 36, 51

4 **A IV**   **Mazurki (A)** op. 6, 7, 17, 24, 30, 33, 41, Mazurek a (Gaillard), Mazurek a (z albumu La France Musicale /Notre Temps/), op. 50, 56, 59, 63

    25 **B I**   **Mazurki (B)** B, G, a, C, F, G, B, As, C, a, g, f

5 **A V**   **Nokturny** op. 9, 15, 27, 32, 37, 48, 55, 62

6 **A VI**   **Polonezy (A)** op. 26, 40, 44, 53, 61

    26 **B II**   **Polonezy (B)** B, g, As, gis, d, f, b, B, Ges

7 **A VII**   **Preludia** op. 28, 45

8 **A VIII** **Ronda** op. 1, 5, 16

9 **A IX**   **Scherza** op. 20, 31, 39, 54

10 **A X**   **Sonaty** op. 35, 58

11 **A XI**   **Walce (A)** op. 18, 34, 42, 64

    27 **B III** **Walce (B)** E, h, Des, As, e, Ges, As, f, a

12 **A XII** **Dzieła różne (A)** Variations brillantes op. 12, Bolero, Tarantela, Allegro de concert, Fantazja op. 49, Berceuse, Barkarola; *suplement* – Wariacja VI z „Hexameronu"

    28 **B IV**   **Dzieła różne (B)** Wariacje E, Sonata c (op. 4)

    29 **B V**   **Różne utwory** Marsz żałobny c, [Warianty] /Souvenir de Paganini/, Nokturn e, Ecossaises D, G, Des, Kontredans, [Allegretto], Lento con gran espressione /Nokturn cis/, Cantabile B, Presto con leggierezza /Preludium As/, Impromptu cis /Fantaisie-Impromptu/, „Wiosna" (wersja na fortepian), Sostenuto /Walc Es/, Moderato /Kartka z albumu/, Galop Marquis, Nokturn c

13 **A XIIIa** **Koncert e-moll** op. 11 na fortepian i orkiestrę (wersja na jeden fortepian)

    30 **B VIa**   **Koncert e-moll** op. 11 na fortepian i orkiestrę (wersja z drugim fortepianem)

14 **A XIIIb** **Koncert f-moll** op. 21 na fortepian i orkiestrę (wersja na jeden fortepian)

    31 **B VIb**   **Koncert f-moll** op. 21 na fortepian i orkiestrę (wersja z drugim fortepianem)

15 **A XIVa** **Utwory koncertowe** na fortepian i orkiestrę op. 2, 13, 14 (wersja na jeden fortepian)

    32 **B VII**   **Utwory koncertowe** na fortepian i orkiestrę op. 2, 13, 14, 22 (wersja z drugim fortepianem)

16 **A XIVb** **Polonez Es-dur** op. 22 na fortepian i orkiestrę (wersja na jeden fortepian)

17 **A XVa**   **Wariacje na temat z** *Don Giovanniego* **Mozarta** op. 2. Partytura

18 **A XVb**   **Koncert e-moll** op. 11. Partytura (wersja historyczna)

    33 **B VIIIa** **Koncert e-moll** op. 11. Partytura (wersja koncertowa)

19 **A XVc**   **Fantazja na tematy polskie** op. 13. Partytura

20 **A XVd**   **Krakowiak** op. 14. Partytura

21 **A XVe**   **Koncert f-moll** op. 21. Partytura (wersja historyczna)

    34 **B VIIIb** **Koncert f-moll** op. 21. Partytura (wersja koncertowa)

22 **A XVf**   **Polonez Es-dur** op. 22. Partytura

23 **A XVI**   **Utwory na fortepian i wiolonczelę** Polonez op. 3, Grand Duo Concertant, Sonata op. 65

    35 **B IX**   **Rondo C-dur** na dwa fortepiany; **Wariacje D-dur** na 4 ręce; *dodatek* – wersja robocza Ronda C-dur (na jeden fortepian)

24 **A XVII** **Trio na fortepian, skrzypce i wiolonczelę** op. 8

    36 **B X**   **Pieśni i piosnki**

37 **Suplement** Utwory częściowego autorstwa Chopina: Hexameron, Mazurki Fis, D, D, C, Wariacje na flet i fortepian; harmonizacje pieśni i tańców: „Mazurek Dąbrowskiego", „Boże, coś Polskę" (Largo), Bourrées G, A, Allegretto A-dur/a-moll

NATIONAL EDITION OF THE WORKS OF FRYDERYK CHOPIN

Plan of the edition

Series A. WORKS PUBLISHED DURING CHOPIN'S LIFETIME

Series B. WORKS PUBLISHED POSTHUMOUSLY

(The titles in square brackets [] have been reconstructed by the National Edition; the titles in slant marks // are still in use today but are definitely, or very probably, not authentic)

1 **A I**	**Ballades** Opp. 23, 38, 47, 52	
2 **A II**	**Etudes** Opp. 10, 25, Three Etudes (Méthode des Méthodes)	
3 **A III**	**Impromptus** Opp. 29, 36, 51	
4 **A IV**	**Mazurkas (A)** Opp. 6, 7, 17, 24, 30, 33, 41, Mazurka in a (Gaillard), Mazurka in a (from the album La France Musicale /Notre Temps/), Opp. 50, 56, 59, 63	25 **B I** **Mazurkas (B)** in B♭, G, a, C, F, G, B♭, A♭, C, a, g, f
5 **A V**	**Nocturnes** Opp. 9, 15, 27, 32, 37, 48, 55, 62	
6 **A VI**	**Polonaises (A)** Opp. 26, 40, 44, 53, 61	26 **B II** **Polonaises (B)** in B♭, g, A♭, g♯, d, f, b♭, B♭, G♭
7 **A VII**	**Preludes** Opp. 28, 45	
8 **A VIII**	**Rondos** Opp. 1, 5, 16	
9 **A IX**	**Scherzos** Opp. 20, 31, 39, 54	
10 **A X**	**Sonatas** Opp. 35, 58	
11 **A XI**	**Waltzes (A)** Opp. 18, 34, 42, 64	27 **B III** **Waltzes (B)** in E, b, D♭, A♭, e, G♭, A♭, f, a
12 **A XII**	**Various Works (A)** Variations brillantes Op. 12, Bolero, Tarantella, Allegro de concert, Fantaisie Op. 49, Berceuse, Barcarolle; *supplement* – Variation VI from "Hexameron"	28 **B IV** **Various Works (B)** Variations in E, Sonata in c (Op. 4)

29 **B V**   **Various Compositions** Funeral March in c, [Variants] /Souvenir de Paganini/, Nocturne in e, Ecossaises in D, G, D♭, Contredanse, [Allegretto], Lento con gran espressione /Nocturne in c♯/, Cantabile in B♭, Presto con leggierezza /Prelude in A♭/, Impromptu in c♯ /Fantaisie-Impromptu/, "Spring" (version for piano), Sostenuto /Waltz in E♭/, Moderato /Feuille d'Album/, Galop Marquis, Nocturne in c

13 **A XIIIa**	**Concerto in E minor** Op. 11 for piano and orchestra (version for one piano)	30 **B VIa** **Concerto in E minor** Op. 11 for piano and orchestra (version with second piano)
14 **A XIIIb**	**Concerto in F minor** Op. 21 for piano and orchestra (version for one piano)	31 **B VIb** **Concerto in F minor** Op. 21 for piano and orchestra (version with second piano)
15 **A XIVa**	**Concert Works** for piano and orchestra Opp. 2, 13, 14 (version for one piano)	32 **B VII** **Concert Works** for piano and orchestra Opp. 2, 13, 14, 22 (version with second piano)
16 **A XIVb**	**Grande Polonaise in E♭ major** Op. 22 for piano and orchestra (version for one piano)	
17 **A XVa**	**Variations on "Là ci darem" from "Don Giovanni"** Op. 2. Score	
18 **A XVb**	**Concerto in E minor** Op. 11. Score (historical version)	33 **B VIIIa** **Concerto in E minor** Op. 11. Score (concert version)
19 **A XVc**	**Fantasia on Polish Airs** Op. 13. Score	
20 **A XVd**	**Krakowiak** Op. 14. Score	
21 **A XVe**	**Concerto in F minor** Op. 21. Score (historical version)	34 **B VIIIb** **Concerto in F minor** Op. 21. Score (concert version)
22 **A XVf**	**Grande Polonaise in E♭ major** Op. 22. Score	
23 **A XVI**	**Works for Piano and Cello** Polonaise Op. 3, Grand Duo Concertant, Sonata Op. 65	35 **B IX** **Rondo in C** for two pianos; **Variations in D** for four hands; *addendum* – working version of Rondo in C (for one piano)
24 **A XVII**	**Piano Trio** Op. 8	36 **B X** **Songs**

37 **Supplement** Compositions partly by Chopin: Hexameron, Mazurkas in F♯, D, D, C, Variations for Flute and Piano; harmonizations of songs and dances: "The Dąbrowski Mazurka", "God who hast embraced Poland" (Largo) Bourrées in G, A, Allegretto in A-major/minor

FRYDERYK CHOPIN
PRELUDES

Performance Commentary
Source Commentary (abridged)

PERFORMANCE COMMENTARY

Notes on the musical text

The v a r i a n t s marked as *ossia* were given this label by Chopin or were added in his hand to pupils' copies; variants without this designation are the result of discrepancies in the texts of authentic versions or an inability to establish an unambiguous reading of the text.

Minor authentic alternatives (single notes, ornaments, slurs, accents, pedal indications, etc.) that can be regarded as variants are enclosed in round brackets ( ), whilst editorial additions are written in square brackets [ ].

Pianists who are not interested in editorial questions, and want to base their performance on a single text, unhampered by variants, are recommended to use the music printed in the principal staves, including all the markings in brackets.

Chopin's original fingering is indicated in large bold-type numerals, **1 2 3 4 5**, in contrast to the editors' fingering which is written in small italic numerals, *1 2 3 4 5*. Wherever authentic fingering is enclosed in parentheses this means that it was not present in the primary sources, but added by Chopin to his pupils' copies. The dashed signs indicating the distribution of parts between the hands come from the editors.

A general discussion on the interpretation of Chopin's works is to be contained in a separate volume: *The Introduction to the National Edition,* in the section entitled *Problems of Performance.*

Abbreviations: R.H. — right hand, L.H. — left hand.

1. Prelude in C major, Op. 28 no. 1

p. 13 The basic R.H. rhythmical figure composed of two triplets of semiquavers seems to suggest an accent on the f i r s t n o t e o f t h e s e c o n d t r i p l e t in each bar, while a variant of the grouping (quintuplet) in bars 18-20, 23 and 25-26 would rather suggest melodic stress on the f i r s t n o t e of the quintuplet. The subtle, but discernible interplay between these two accents may be an important element in the expression of the entire prelude.

2. Prelude in A minor, Op. 28 no. 2

p. 14 L.H. T w o v o i c e s, as indicated by Chopin in the first two bars, are continued through the entire prelude. This should be realized via *legatissimo* and a slight detachment of the inner voice (*B-A#-B-G*), and *legato possibile* of the outer.

Chopin wrote p e d a l s i g n s only for bars 18-19 but this does not mean that the pedal is to be used here for the very first time. The editors believe that it can be added from the beginning:
— in bars 1-12 on every quaver (facilitating *legato* for the L.H.); at the beginning of bar 6 the pedal can be kept down over the first crotchet;
— in bars 13-16 for longer, on every crotchet;
— in bars 18-19 as indicated on the score.

Bars 5, 10, 17 & 20 R.H. The editors propose the following rhythmical solution of quaver with grace-note ♪♪♩ (in bars 5 and 10 the grace-note should be played simultaneously with the fourth L.H. quaver). Cf. *Source Commentary.*

Bar 22 R.H. The first note of the arpeggio (*d*) should be struck together with the L.H. octave.

3. Prelude in G major, Op. 28 no. 3

Chopin omitted to put in any p e d a l m a r k s but that does not indicate that the pedal is forbidden altogether. The editors believe it is most natural to add the pedal at the beginning of each bar and release it gradually, "gently", more or less in mid-bar. In bar 30 it is best to pedal the first and third beat. The pedal depressed at the beginning of bar 31 can be lifted after the figuration ends on the first note of bar 32.

p. 15 *Bars 8, 10, 18 & 24* R.H. The lower note of the arpeggiated chord should be struck together with the first semiquaver played by the L.H.

p. 16 *Bars 32-33* It is better to play the arpeggios in a continuous fashion, i.e. *b* with the R.H. after *g* with the L.H.

4. Prelude in E minor, Op. 28 no. 4

p. 17 *Bars 11 & 19* R.H. The signs written most probably by Chopin on one of his pupils' copies indicate that the grace-note should be played simultaneously with the penultimate L.H. chord. However, it is not clear what rhythmical value it should have (cf. *Source Commentary*). The editors believe that it should not be shorter than a semiquaver (♪♩ = ♫♩.) and not longer than a quaver (♪♩ = ♫♩), and the best version would be a quaver in the triplet (♪♩ = ♫♩). (Cf. note to *Prelude in A minor, Op. 28 no. 2*, bars 5, 10, 17 & 20).

5. Prelude in D major, Op. 28 no. 5

p. 18 *Bars 10-11 & 26-27.* A facilitated version of the L.H. part:

Bars 13-16 & 29-32 R.H. On contemporary pianos (in Chopin's time the keys were slightly slenderer) the figurations of these bars are easier to play holding down *b¹* in bars 13-16 and *g¹* in 29-32 only for the duration of 3 semiquavers (as ♪.).

6. Prelude in B minor, Op. 28 no. 6

R.H. In bar 1, the articulation and expression markings given by Chopin over the upper voice are exemplar and so they should be applied to all analogous motifs throughout the *Prelude*. Repeating them on the third beat of bar 22 will give a special emphasis to the seventh *a¹*.

p. 19 *Bar 7* R.H. It seems more in style to play the grace-note together with *f#¹* from the lower voice and the L.H. *d*. Choosing the arpeggio which figures in parentheses, it should be played thus:

. In this case, it would seem more in character to strike *f#¹* with the *d*.

p. 20 *Bars 23-26* L.H. The original pedaling—one pedal through the four final bars—sounds just as good on contemporary pianos. However, wishing to avoid the sound of the semitone *d-c#* in the final harmony one can play as follows:

2

7. Prelude in A major, Op. 28 no. 7

p. 21 *Bar 12* This simplified version for a smaller hand was written by

Chopin on a pupil's copy:
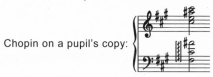

8. Prelude in F sharp minor, Op. 28 no. 8

p. 24 *Final bar* Arpeggio with grace-note solutions:

9. Prelude in E major, Op. 28 no. 9

p. 25 Throughout the *Prelude*:
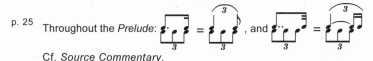

Cf. *Source Commentary*.

Bars 3 & 4 L.H. The trill beginning in bar 3:

A#₁ simultaneously with the R.H. chord on the fourth beat. Analogously in bar 4.

10. Prelude in C sharp minor, Op. 28 no. 10

p. 26 *Bar 7* L.H. Trill beginning:
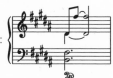

C## simultaneously with *f##-a#* in the R.H.

11. Prelude in B major, Op. 28 no. 11

p. 27 *Bar 21* The execution of the grace-note:

Bars 25-27 Chopin wanted the three final bars to be played on one pedal which may sound too heavy on contemporary pianos. The editors suggest the following solution:

With a gentle change of pedal in the last bar this gives a sound which closely resembles that intended by Chopin.

12. Prelude G sharp minor, Op. 28 no. 12

F i n g e r i n g :
In bars 1-4 and in analogous ones it is possible to use different fingering:

bars 1-4

bars 11-13

bars 51-52

To simplify the R.H. part, the original division of chords between the two hands can be altered in several places, switching the lowermost of notes placed on the upper stave (e.g. on the third beat of bar 7) to L.H. It is particularly comfortable to do this in bars 54, 56 and 57.

13. Prelude in F sharp major, Op. 28 no. 13

p. 31 *Bar 1 ff.* L.H. The *legato* description under the bottom stave probably means "harmonic legato" (holding down components of a harmony with the fingers). Its precise execution was easier on pianos in Chopin's time, which had narrower keys:

If this is impossible to play because of a small hand span, the following fingering and pedaling may be applied, taking care of the articulation (as *legato* as possible) of the notes played with the first finger:

Bar 1

Bar 6

In bar 1 and analogous bars some notes may be taken over by the R.H.:

The following, simpler solution gives a very approximate sound effect to the original:

(care should be taken to change pedal gently on the *f#* notes).

Bar 7 R.H.  *f#¹* together with *G#* in the L.H.

p. 32 *Bars 33-36* R.H. The execution of the chord at the beginning of

bar 33:  , and by analogy in subsequent bars.

The editors advocate that Chopin's p e d a l i n g is preserved (cf. *Source Commentary*) with one addendum—on the last beat of bar 33 it is better to change the pedal than to release it.

The pedal marks (in brackets) added over the top stave follow Chopin's indications from previous bars. The marks added under the bottom stave are a practical suggestion which would preserve the continuity of both main R.H. melodic lines.

14. Prelude in E flat minor, Op. 28 no. 14

s. 33   Chopin's omission of p e d a l i n g m a r k s does not indicate that the pedal should not be used. The editors suggest:
— in bars 1, 2, 5, 6, 11 & 12—pedal depressed gently (not too fast) at the beginning and gently released in mid-bar,
— in remaining bars—one pedal for each half of the bar.

15. Prelude in D flat major, Op. 28 no. 15

p. 34   *Bar 3 & analog.* Pedal change on the second beat, although not marked by Chopin in bars 26 and 78, is indicated for contemporary instruments in each of these places. According to Chopin's notation, the player should take care to sustain the third ab-c^1 with the L.H.

p. 35   *Bars 38-39 & analog.* Because of the grace-note in the bass the pedal can be depressed a crotchet earlier than Chopin indicated.

p. 37   *Bars 81-83* The pedal release signs [✻] in bars 81 and 83 describe the shortest and the longest of possible holds on a pedal depressed at the beginning of bar 81.

16. Prelude in B flat minor, Op. 28 no. 16

p. 38   *Bars 2-8 & 18-25* The original pedaling should be preserved, as it gives a "torrential" sound effect both on pianos from the time of Chopin and contemporary instruments (cf. *Sonata in B♭ minor* Op. 35, first movement, bars 5-15). Chopin used this pedaling quite consciously, probably after having experimented with it (in bars 2-3 the autograph shows deletions of earlier markings denoting a pedal change for every half-bar). The short pedal applied by most pianists on the first and third beat in these bars reduces to a considerable degree the effect intended by Chopin.

17. Prelude in A flat major, Op. 28 no. 17

p. 43   *Bar 38* L.H. If there are difficulties in spanning the chords in the second part of the bar, the topmost notes, ab^1, are better played with the R.H.

p. 44   *Bars 43 & 47* The arpeggio with grace-notes in bar 43:

Anticipated grace-notes (quaver b^1 together with the L.H. chord). Per analogiam in bar 47.

Bar 56 R.H. The grace-notes are easier played with the following fingering: , adding on the bottom note of the chords, ab^1, to the L.H. part.
The first of the grace-notes, f^2, should be struck together with d^2 and the L.H. chord.

p. 45   *Bars 65-87* Clean changes of harmony and at the same time a longer sounding pedal point Ab_1 can be achieved by a rapid change of pedal in the positions marked. One can also apply the middle pedal, using it to catch the Ab_1 in bar 67 and sustain it until the end of the piece.

Bars 88-90 A clean sonority of the ultimate A♭-major chord together with its fundamental Ab_1 can also be achieved without the use of the middle pedal (see previous note). This would require a "mute" hold on the bass note:

18. Prelude in F minor, Op. 28 no. 18

p. 47   *Bar 18* The trill should be started on the main note.

21. Prelude in B flat major, Op. 28 no. 21

P e d a l i n g : In the basic figure of the accompaniment the pedal should be lifted gradually, with a gentle motion. In this way the pedal can be released completely a little later than would arise from Chopin's notation.

p. 52   *Bars 18-19* On contemporary pianos, in order to prolong the sound of the bass note Gb_1 it is possible not to change the pedal when passing from one bar to the other.

22. Prelude in G minor, Op. 28 no. 22

p. 54   *Bars 1-4, 9-12 & 35-38* The interpretation of L.H. slurring which is inconsistent in the sources may give rise to doubts. The editors believe that the differences in slurring analogous fragments do not have to imply differences in execution. The slurs indicate rather the articulation *legato* than energetics of the octave phrases. In practice the following unification of Chopin's slurring in these bars may be proposed:

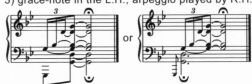

This interpretation seems supported by the ⇒ signs (diminuendo or long accent). These concern both hands and above all signify accents: on the L.H. octave which begins the bar and the R.H. chord which follows (a specific "polyaccentuation" of Chopin's).

p. 55   *Final bar* The two slurs before the last chord denote its division between the two hands. Both slurs or just the top one could also signify arpeggio. Considering these options, the bar can be executed as follows:
1) grace-note, followed by an unarpeggiated chord in both hands,
2) continuous arpeggio with both hands (from G_1 to g^1),
3) grace-note in the L.H., arpeggio played by R.H.:

23. Prelude in F major, Op. 28 no. 23

p. 56   *Bars 2, 6, 10 & 18* L.H. The execution of the trill with grace-notes

in bar 2:

Per analogiam in bars 6, 10 & 18.

24. Prelude in D minor, Op. 28 no. 24

L e f t   h a n d . One should take care to hold the second semiquaver, as indicated by Chopin in the figures of the initial bars. This is fundamentally important for a firm hold of the wide position and, should be applied throughout the prelude whenever possible.

p. 57   *Bars 7 & 25* R.H. The best solution for the ornament in bar 7:

By analogy in bar 25.

p. 58   *Bars 10 & 28* R.H. The execution of the trill with grace-notes in

bar 10:

Analogously in bar 28.

Bars 12, 16, 30 & 34 R.H. Trills should begin with the main note.

25. Prelude in C sharp minor, Op. 45

The variants of Chopin's p e d a l i n g (markings in or without parentheses) should be read as follows:
— in bars 5-6 & analogous, the (❀) and ❀ marks describe the earliest and the latest moment to release a pedal depressed at the beginning of the L.H. figuration. In practice, one may suggest a gentle and gradual release in-between the two signs;
— in bars 8-9 the pedal should be depressed on the last quaver of bar 8 or at the beginning of bar 9 and held at least towards the end of bar 9, and similarly in all analogous places;
— in bars 35-36 it is left to the discretion of the performer whether to change the pedal in the middle of bar 35; if so, then the editors believe that it is better to start the new pedal on the sixth quaver of the bar; and whichever version is preferred, the moment of release should be as for bars 5-6 above;

p. 63   *Bar 33* Deciding to release the pedal in mid-bar, one may help keep the bass by applying "harmonic legato" (fingers sustain components of the harmony):

An analogous device may be used in bar 57.

p. 66   *Bar 84* L.H. To supplement Chopin's pedaling, the editors suggest "harmonic legato" (see above), by holding the sixth quaver *c#* until the pedal is depressed on *a*.

Bars 88-89 To preserve the continuous sonority on contemporary pianos it is better not to change the pedal when passing from the one bar to the other.

Jan Ekier
Paweł Kamiński

5

SOURCE COMMENTARY /ABRIDGED/

Introductory comments

The following commentary sets out in an abridged form the principles of editing the musical text of particular works and discusses the most important discrepancies between the authentic sources; furthermore, it draws attention to departures from the authentic text which are most frequently encountered in the collected editions of Chopin's music compiled after his death. A separately published *Source Commentary* contains a detailed description of the sources, their filiation, justification of the choice of primary sources, a thorough presentation of the differences between them and a reproduction of characteristic fragments.

Abbreviations: R.H. – right hand, L.H. – left hand. The sign → symbolizes a connection between sources; it should be read "and ... based on it".

1-24. Preludes, Op. 28

Sources

A Autograph of all 24 Preludes, sent from Majorca on January 22, 1839 to Julian Fontana for copying (National Library, Warsaw). **A** served as the basis for the first French edition. Many deletions and corrections, a large part of which concern performance directions, represent the work devoted by Chopin to **A**. In spite of this, **A** does contain a variety of errors and inaccuracies in notation, mostly a considerable number of omissions of accidentals in some of the preludes.

FC Copy of **A** made by Julian Fontana (lost, photocopy held by the Chopin Society in Warsaw). **FC** served as the basis for the first German edition. As a whole, the copier duplicated the **A** text carefully, nonetheless making a number of mistakes, the gravest of which are omissions of entire bars in *Preludes in G# minor* no. 12 and *in Bb* no. 21. Chopin did not correct **FC**.
Certain pencilled markings on some of the Preludes (mainly filling in the chromatic signs) were made by the long-time owner of the manuscript, Hermann Scholtz, who based his own edition of the *Preludes* (Peters, Leipzig 1879) on the **FC**.

Individual manuscripts of eight preludes (nos. 2, 3, 4, 6, 7, 9, 17 and 20) are described as additional sources in reference to each prelude.

FE1 First French edition, Ad. Catelin et Cⁱᵉ (Adᵉ.C.(560) & Cⁱᵉ), Paris, August 1839. **FE1** is based on **A** and was not revised by Chopin. Corrections, which included supplemented accidentals and pedaling, were added by J. Fontana (see quotes *about the Preludes...* which precede the musical text).

FE2 Second impression of **FE1** (same company and number) printed not long after the first. **FE2** contains some alterations, mostly corrections of the errors of **FE1**. Most probably they were also made by J. Fontana although it is not possible to entirely exclude the participation of Chopin, indirect as it may have been. There are copies of **FE2** which have differing prices on the cover.

FE3 Third impression of **FE1**, Brandus et Cⁱᵉ (B et Cⁱᵉ 4594), Paris, December 1846, and later reimpressions. The musical text is identical to **FE2**.

FE = **FE1**, **FE2** and **FE3**.

FED, FEJ, FES, FESch—teaching copies of **FE** with Chopin's remarks on fingering, performance directions, variants, corrections of printing errors:
  FED—copy from the collection of Chopin's pupil, Camille Dubois (Bibliothèque Nationale, Paris),
  FEJ—copy from the collection of Chopin's sister, Ludwika Jędrzejewicz (Chopin Society, Warsaw),
  FES—copy from the collection of Chopin's pupil, Jane Stirling (Bibliothèque Nationale, Paris),
  FESch—copy from the collection of Chopin's pupil, Marie de Scherbatoff (Houghton Library, New York).

The set of Preludes containing annotations in Chopin's hand or which may have come from Chopin is different in the case of each of the above collections:
  FED—*Preludes* nos. 1, 3, 4, 6, 7, 9, 11-13, 15, 17-21, 23 & 24,
  FES—*Preludes* nos. 2-4, 6, 7, 9, 11, 13-15, 17, 20, 21 & 24,
  FEJ—*Preludes* nos. 4, 6, 9, 11, 15, 17 & 21,
  FESch—*Preludes* nos. 7, 11 & 16.

GE1 First German edition, Breitkopf & Härtel (6088), Leipzig, September 1839. **GE1** is based on **FC**, it contains many adjustments and errors. Chopin took no part in the preparation of **GE1**. There are copies of **GE1** which have differing covers, and the edition was also published in a version of 4 fascicules containing 6 preludes each.

GE2 Second impression of **GE1** (same company and number), circa 1868, with many of the errors corrected and many arbitrary alterations introduced.

GE3 Third impression of **GE1** (same company and number) with further small changes. There are copies of both versions of **GE3** (complete opus or 4 fascicules) and also with a new price imprinted on the cover after 1872.

GE = **GE1**, **GE2** and **GE3**.

EE1 First English edition, divided into two fascicules, one with 14 and the other with 10 preludes, Wessel & Cᵒ (W & Cᵒ 3098 and 3099), London, January 1840. **EE1** is based on **FE2**, with some adjustments, e. g. the fingering has been added in some of the preludes. Chopin had no part in preparing the edition.

EE2 Second impression of **EE1** (same company and number), after 1855, with small alterations. The editors had access only to book 1 of **EE2**.

EE = **EE1** and **EE2**.

Editorial Principles
We base this edition on **A**. In some places, where one might suspect Chopin to have had made a mistake, we compare **A** with manuscripts of the particular *Preludes*. We have taken into consideration the annotations on pupils' copies made by Chopin or which may have come from Chopin.

Dedication
In **A** (→**FC**→**GE**) there is the dedication: "à son ami J. C. Kessler". However, in March 1839 Chopin wrote in a letter to Fontana: "I very much want my Preludes to be dedicated to Pleyel [...]. Nothing to Kessler. [...] Tell Probst [who acted as agent between Chopin and the German publisher] about the changed dedication". The alteration was made in **FE** (→**EE**) and also the **FC** was appropriately amended. In this situation, the appearance of **GE** with the original dedication to Kessler can be explained by misunderstanding or reluctance to change a title page which—perhaps—was complete. It cannot be excluded that Chopin took advantage of the fact that for commercial reasons circulation of particular editions was restricted, and decided to honour two patrons with one opus—a Frenchman with the French edition and a German with the German one.

1. Prelude in C major, Op. 28 no. 1

Sources and editorial principles
See above *1-24. Preludes, Op. 28.*

p. 13 *Bars 18-20, 23 & 25-26* R.H. In **GE2** the original quintuplets were altered to the same rhythm as in the remaining bars.

Bar 34 L.H. In **FE** beside the three notes sustained from the previous bar there is an erroneous *E* note.

2. Prelude in A minor, Op. 28 no. 2

Sources and editorial principles
See *1-24. Preludes, Op. 28* on page 6.

Additional sources
As   A shorthand sketch of the whole *Prelude* in a version very close to the ultimate one (private collection, photocopy at the Chopin Society, Warsaw).
CGS   Copy made by George Sand probably from **FE**1 (private collection, photocopy in: *Korespondencja Chopina z George Sand i jej dziećmi*, ed. K. Kobylańska, Warsaw 1981).

p. 14   *Bar 1* **EE** and some of the later collected editions arbitrarily changed the time signature from ¢ to ℂ.

Bars 1-2 The notation of **A**:  has been reduced in **FE** (→**EE**) to one part as in the following bars. The probable reason for the simplification, most likely not in line with what Chopin intended, was the complex graphical arrangement of the original script, difficult to render in print.

Bars 5, 10, 17 & 20 R.H. The grace-notes are given here as according to **A** (→**FE**→**EE**). In **FC** (→**GE**) they have been written as crossed ones. Such inaccuracies in recording ornaments are typical for Fontana's copies. In **FE**S Chopin crossed the grace-notes in bars 17 and 20, probably correcting erroneous execution during a lesson. Cf. *Performance Commentary*.

3. Prelude in G major, Op. 28 no. 3

Sources and editorial principles
See *1-24. Preludes, Op. 28* on page 6.

Additional source
FCI   Fontana's copy of a lost autograph with an earlier edition of the *Prelude* (Chopin Society, Warsaw).

p. 15   *Bar 1* In some of the later collected editions, the time signature has been arbitrarily altered from ¢ to ℂ.

p. 16   *Bar 17* R.H. In **FC** the second half of the bar has a mistaken rhythm ♩. ♪ . In the **GE** this has been changed to ♩.. ♪ which is rhythmically correct but inconsistent with Chopin's original notation in **A** (→**FE**→**EE**).

Bars 22-23 R.H. Some of the later collected editions arbitrarily tied the notes *e¹* and *g¹*.

Bar 31 **FC** (→**GE**) features an erroneous *cresc.* to describe the dynamics. The description also figures in **FC**I, so it must have been the original concept for this bar, later altered by Chopin to *dim.* which figures in **A** (→**FE**→**EE**).

4. Prelude in E minor, Op. 28 no. 4

Sources and editorial principles
See *1-24. Preludes, Op. 28* on page 6.

Additional sources
As   As for *Prelude in A minor*, Op. 28 no. 2.
CGS   Copy made by George Sand probably from **FE**1 (private collection, photocopy in: K. Kobylańska, *Rękopisy utworów Chopina*, Cracow 1977).

p. 17   *Upbeat* The sign ***p*** was overlooked in **FC** (→**GE**).

Bar 11 L.H. **GE** has a *B-d♯-a* chord erroneously repeated throughout the bar.

Bars 11 & 19 R.H. In **FE**D there are markings which possibly indicate how to play the grace-notes. The sign in bar 19 seems to equate ♪♩ with ♪♩. Cf. *Performance Commentary*.

Bar 12 R.H. The *ossia* variant comes from **FE**J.

Bar 16 R.H. Sources have no accidentals under the turn. This is most obviously an omission by Chopin and it points indirectly at *g♯♯¹* (sounding as *a¹*) which may have seemed to Chopin as not needing any sign.

5. Prelude in D major, Op. 28 no. 5

Sources and editorial principles
See *1-24. Preludes, Op. 28* on page 6.

p. 18   *Bars 13-16 & 29-32* R.H. The crotchet stems added on to the notes *b¹* in bars 13-16 and *g¹* in bars 29-32 are here given after **A**. Because of deletions in **A** the stems disappear from **FC** (→**GE**) and **FE** (→**EE**).

Bar 16 R.H. In **FC**, bars 15-16 are marked as a repetition of bar 14, because the copyist overlooked ♮ written before the last note in bar 16 of **A** (in **A** only bar 15 is marked this way, bar 16 is written out in notes). Hence the erroneous final *a♯²* in this bar in **GE**.

6. Prelude in B minor, Op. 28 no. 6

Sources and editorial principles
See *1-24. Preludes, Op. 28* on page 6.

Additional source
CGS   As for *Prelude in E minor*, Op. 28 no. 4.

p. 19   *Bar 7* R.H. The arpeggio is featured in **FE**D.

p. 20   *Bars 12-14* **A** (→**FC**→**GE**) lacks the naturals lowering c♯ to c (in all octaves). This has been revised in **FE** (→**EE**).

Bars 13, 15-17 & 20-21 The dynamic signs contained in parentheses come from **FE**S. The variant ***pp*** from bar 13 is featured in **FE**J.

Bar 19 R.H. The second crotchet of the lower part is *c♯¹-f♯¹* according to **A**. **FC** (→**GE**) and **FE** (→**EE**) contain *c♯¹-g¹* (as in the following bar). The mistake of the copyist and the **FE**'s engraver could have been provoked either by the similarity of bars 19 & 20, or the slightly raised position of the upper note in **A**, suggesting an interval of a second.
The voice-leading which is analogous to bar 15 also speaks in favour of *f♯¹*.

Bars 22-23 L.H. The tie on the *B₁* appears in **A** (→**FC**→**GE**, →**FE** →**EE**). It has been crossed out in **FE**S. In **FE**J there is fingering which suggests a repetition of the sound in bar 23—the numeral **5** written under *B₁* in bar 22 as well as *B₁* and *B* in bar 23 (Chopin pointed to similar use of the fifth finger in several other compositions, e. g. in the *Nocturnes in C♯ minor* Op. 27 no. 1, bars 13-14 and *in B* Op. 32 no. 1, bars 26 & 36). It seems advisable to play *B₁* in bar 23 in view of the rhythm of the basic motif and the original pedaling.

7. Prelude in A major, Op. 28 no. 7

Sources and editorial principles
See *1-24. Preludes, Op. 28* on page 6.

Additional sources
CXI Copy by unknown copyist (Österreiche Nationalbibliothek, Vienna) which may carry the earlier version of the prelude's character and tempo description—*Lento misterioso*. This possibility is also indicated by the fact that *Lento* was initially marked on **A**, then crossed out and replaced by *Andantino*.
CGS As for *Prelude in A minor, Op. 28 no. 2*.

p. 21   *Bar 11* R.H. In **A** (→FC→**GE**1, →**FE**) the beginning of the bar omits ♯ which raises d^2 to $d\#^2$. In **FE**S and **FE**Sch the sign has been replaced.

Bar 12 The simplified version of the chord given in the *Performance Commentary* was inscribed in **FE**S.

Bar 13 R.H. On the third beat in **A** (→**FE**→**EE**) ♮ is missing to lower $a\#^1$ to a^1. This is an obvious mistake corrected in F**C** (→**GE**) and **FE**D.

Bar 15 In F**C** (→**GE**), the third crotchet erroneously repeats the previous chord $e\text{-}a\text{-}e^1$.

8. Prelude in F sharp minor, Op. 28 no. 8

Sources and editorial principles
See *1-24. Preludes, Op. 28* on page 6.
In this *Prelude* we tacitly replace the exceptionally large number of accidentals obviously omitted from **A** (replacements have also been made in lesser or greater degree in the remaining sources).

p. 21   *Bar 4* R.H. **A** (→FC→**GE**) erroneously omits ♮ before the fourth demisemiquaver of the last group.

p. 22   *Bars 6 & 20* R.H. In some of the later collected editions the final demisemiquaver in the second group has been arbitrarily altered from a^2 to $f\#^2$. In both bars in **A** the figure is fully written out in notes (with no abbreviations) and carries no corrections, thus excluding any possibility that the composer could have made a mistake. Often Chopin increased the span of figurations basically contained within an octave, for instance in *Preludes in E* no. 9, bars 2, 4 & 8, *in Db* no. 15, bars 70 & 72-75, *in F* no. 23, bar 14 or *Etudes in Ab* op. 10 no. 10, bars 61-62 & 68, *in F* Op. 25 no. 3, bars 18 & 20. Chopin's use of a^2 in this position was probably intended to avoid the false relation $f\#^2\text{-}f^1$ with the subsequent note played by the L.H.

Bar 9 L.H. The main text is a version read literally from sources. However, the crossings and corrections on this figure in **A** allow for the assumption that Chopin forgot to write ♮ lowering $g\#$ to g, especially if he made the changes after he had written the subsequent figure, where there is a g (with ♮). We cite this possibility (which in effect gives a version analogous to bar 10) in the variant.

Bar 13 R.H. In **A** (→FC→**GE**, →**FE**1), there is no ♮ to precede the third demisemiquaver in the third group. This is clearly an omission of Chopin's—in the great majority of groups the third and fifth demisemiquaver form a semitone. ♮ has been added in **FE**2 (→**EE**).

p. 23   *Bar 17* All sources cite b^1 on the third demisemiquaver of the second group. This is a remainder of the original version—initially in **A**, in the first two figures of bars 15-18, the third demisemiquaver was bb^1. Chopin replaced it 7 times (out of 8) with ab^1. He must have forgotten the said note as he made the corrections— this is additionally proved by the fact that he left it without ♭.

Bar 21 R.H. In **A** (→FC→**GE**), the fourth demisemiquaver of the third group is g^2 as it is not preceded by an accidental. This is an obvious omission by Chopin corrected in **FE** (→**EE**).

p. 24   *Bar 23* R.H. In **A** (→FC→**GE**1), there is no accidental before the fourth demisemiquaver of the third group, thus it should be read as $d\#^3$. In **FE** (→**EE**) – and also **GE**2 (→**GE**3) – ♮ has been added (d^3). In this case Fontana's addition in **FE** seems matter for discussion, since a number of musical as well as source arguments would support $d\#^3$:
— deletions in neighbouring bars prove that Chopin was watching the chromatic signs in **A**;
— d^1 and d^2 after the C♯-minor chord in bar 24 have been marked with naturals by Chopin in the R.H part where the sign is necessary as well as the L.H, where it is only a precautionary measure;
— a similar combination of sounds describing the major chord was used by Chopin at the end of bar 24 (a^1 and $c\#^2$ with a G-major chord). However, since it is not possible to exclude that Chopin accidentally omitted ♮ here (and so that Fontana was right in **FE**) we give both versions, nonetheless with priority to the **A** version with $d\#^3$.

9. Prelude in E major, Op. 28 no. 9

Sources and editorial principles
See *1-24. Preludes, Op. 28* on page 6.

Additional source:
CGS As for *Prelude in A minor, Op. 28 no. 2*.

We recreate the notation of dotted rhythms against triplets as it appears in **A** (→FC) and as it was used by Chopin in all of his works (see the chapter devoted to this matter in Jan Ekier's *Introduction to the National Edition, Editorial Problems*) In **FE** (→**EE**) and **GE** the semiquavers have been moved beyond the third note of the triplet. Newer editions (Henle Verlag from 1956, Peters from 1985) return to Chopin's version. The first artist to record the authentic rhythmical version was Maurizio Pollini (Deutsche Grammophon Gesellschaft 1975).
This problem relates to the doubts over the manner of separating the top voice. We adopt the notation which most frequently appears in **A**, where the top notes of chords belong to both voices simultaneously, thus the upper part becomes merely an individual element of the figuration and not a wholly independent part.

p. 25   *Bar 7* On the third beat in **A** (→FC), naturals lowering f♯ to f are missing. They have been replaced in **FE** (→**EE**) and **GE**. The version with f♯, although acceptable as it sounds, is highly unlikely because of the unusual spelling of the F♯/G♭-major chord. Chopin did not object to the naturals as they appear in print in the three pupils' copies which carry his annotations.

Bar 9 R.H. Added octaves in the bass part seem appropriate because of the shape of the motif (cf. bar 1) which is repeated in octaves in the following two bars (10-11).

Bar 12 R.H. **FE** (→**EE**) omits the tie linking b notes in the final chord and preceding third.
L.H. **GE** incorrectly recreates the tie on B_1 as a slur linking this note and the final E_1.

10. Prelude in C sharp minor, Op. 28 no. 10

Sources and editorial principles
See *1-24. Preludes, Op. 28* on page 6.

p. 26   *Bar 7* R.H. Chopin mistakenly dotted the minim $g\#$.

Bar 18 R.H. **A** (→**FE**→**EE**) gives f♯ as the lower note of the semiquaver chord. The note is written somewhat imprecisely in **A**, so it has been mistakenly read as g♯ in F**C** (→**GE**).

11. Prelude in B major, Op. 28 no. 11

Sources and editorial principles
See *1-24. Preludes, Op. 28* on page 6.

p. 27 *Bar 21* The grace-note, its tie and a slur have been recreated following **A**. Remaining sources deform the notation of the bar:
— in **FC** (→**GE**) the tie and slur have been omitted, and the grace-note is written as ♪;
— in **FE** (→**EE**) the slur which crosses the tie in **A** was read erroneously as a f sign.

Bar 23 At the marked place **FE**D contains a pencilled line crossing the slur.

12. Prelude in G sharp minor, Op. 28 no. 12

Sources and editorial principles
See *1-24. Preludes, Op. 28* on page 6.

p. 28 *Bar 12* R.H. The slurs follow **A** (→**FC**). They were possibly considered illogical by engravers (proof-readers?) and altered:
— in **FE** (→**EE**) one slur ends on the fourth quaver in bar 12 and the next begins at the sixth quaver in the bar,
— in **GE** the first slur has been extended to the final quaver of bar 12.

Bars 21-22 L.H. **FE** (→**EE**) is missing the tie on *B*.

Bars 21-22 & 25-26 R.H. Slurs signifying *tenuto* over minims in bars 21 and 25 have been arbitrarily altered in **GE** to ties on *b¹* in bars 21-22 and *a¹* in bars 25-26. Similar slurs have been omitted in bars 22 and 26.

Bars 21, 24 & 25 L.H. Some of the later collected editions arbitrarily tied the top notes of the fifths which close the bars: the *f#* in bars 21-22 and *e* in 24-25 & 25-26.

Bars 23-24 R.H In all sources the top notes in bar 23 are *c#²* (♮ pencilled on **FC** is a later and alien addition—see the notes on **FC**). In many later collected editions, possibly to avoid a cross relation with *c¹* in bar 24, the notes have been changed to *c²*. While there is small probability that Chopin mistakenly omitted ♮ in bar 23, there are reasons to question the purpose of ♮ to lower *c#¹* to *c¹* in bar 24. This is a reconstruction based on an analysis of the music's layout and visible corrections, of the three-stage notation process in **A**, bars 23-26:

Stage 1:

In this version, subsequent keys in bars 21-28 are grouped in regular sets of two bars, the version also avoids the above said cross relation *c#²-c¹*. *c#¹* in bar 24 also helps explain (easier fingering) the exceptional rhythmical value of the crotchet *a¹* in this bar—in all analogous places (in bars 21-22, 25-26 and particularly in bar 28 which closes the four-bar fragment) there are minims.

Stage 2:

Possibly the above alteration to bar 24 was introduced by Chopin—misled by the lack of a full notation in bar 26—in the belief that bars 24-25 are the first two bars of a four-bar clause, i. e. 25-26.

Stage 3:

Chopin relinquished the idea to raise to *d#¹* the top note on the fourth quaver in bars 24-26.

The basic conclusion from the above reconstruction is that the corrections made by Chopin in bars 24-25 (stages 2 and 3) were probably intended for bars 25-26; this does not impact on the sound of the latter but it proves wrong the version of bar 24 which figures in **A**. Chopin's intentions would probably be answered by the version described in the first of the above examples (with *c#¹*). That is why we give it as an acceptable variant of this bar.

p. 29 *Bar 30* R.H. In **A** (→**FC,FE**) there are no chromatic signs before the last octave. The possibilities are two:
— Chopin was thinking of the octave *d¹-d²* and forgot to write ♮ at the lower note of the octave:

— Chopin was thinking of the octave *d#¹-d#²* and forgot ♯ before the upper note of the octave:

An analysis of the notation of the third crotchet in bar 30 in **A**, including the deletion preceding the final octave in the bar, does not turn the balance to favour any of the above versions. In our opinion, the lower notes of the octaves were added at a later time, Chopin began writing ♯ before *d#¹* but realized it was not necessary and then mistakenly crossed out ♯ he had placed before at the upper note.
A stylistic analysis of bars 29-32 does clearly support the second version: bars 31-32 are basically a repetition of bars 29-30; in the one pair as well as in the other the harmonic progression leads to the E-minor chord (at the beginning of bar 31 and 33); thus it is much more probable that corresponding chords in both pairs are—apart from the first one—identical.
In **GE**1 and **EE** there is ♮ added which lowers *d#¹* to *d¹*, in **GE**2 ♯ has been placed before both notes in the discussed octave.

Bar 32 L.H. In **FE** (→**EE**) the tie on *f#* has been omitted.

Bar 36 R.H. **A** (→**FE**→**EE**) gives the octave *g##¹-g##²* on the fifth quaver of the bar. **FC** (→**GE**) also has there the crotchet *f#²*. This place was corrected by Chopin at least four times in **A**. Among the many deletions he left the version with *f#²* (as in **FC**), then he scratched the note out, possibly so as not to add yet another confusing deletion. However, some of the ink did remain and this may have misled the copyist.
This is a typical example of Chopin's economy with sound. Traces of removing well-sounding but unnecessary notes can also be seen in other places in this prelude (e. g. the crossed-out crotchets *a#¹* on the second and third beat in bar 39).

p. 30 *Bar 64* **FE** (→**EE**) contains a continuous pedal held throughout the bar. We omit this marking, added by Fontana in his proof-reading of **FE**1.

Bar 70 LH The majority of later collected editions change the first octave from *E-e* to *G#-g#*. The deletions and corrections in **A** prove that Chopin did try out several versions (including the *G#-g#* octave) and wrote down *E-e* as the final one.

Bar 78-79 These bars are missing from **FC** (→**GE**). This is a typical error ("haplography") possibly caused by their similarity to bars 76-77. Cf. commentary to the *Prelude in B♭* Op. 28 no. 21, bar 54.

13. Prelude in F sharp major, Op. 28 no. 13

Sources and editorial principles
See *1-24. Preludes, Op. 28* on page 6.

p. 31   *Bar 1* According to sources, the time signature is 3/2. This is Chopin's mistake (the correct metre should be 6/4) probably related to a changed notation: Chopin began to write the *Prelude* in a 6/8 metre and with rhythmical values halved.

Bars 4 & 12 R.H. We have adopted a value of o in bar 4 and o· in bar 12 for the *c#¹* which appears at the beginning of these bars in **A** (→**FE**→**EE**). In view of the original pedaling both forms are equal. In bar 4 **FC** has only ρ· and **GE** has the erroneous value in both bars.

Bar 6 R.H. Instead of the rest which closes the bar, **FC** (→**GE**) erroneously has dots to lengthen the second chord.

Bar 7 & 9 R.H. In **GE**2 the grace-note in bar 7 is ♪. In some of the later collected editions this non-authentic grace-note form also appears in bar 9.

p. 32   *Bar 22* R.H. Part of the later collected editions give the first *e#¹* in the lower voice replaced with a quaver rest.

Bar 31 R.H. In **FES** at the end of the bar there is an indistinct pencilled addition, possibly made by Chopin. It can be read as the following variant:

(when the added small notes are played as semiquavers—the first one simultaneously with the L.H. *b*—they create an analogy with the motifs in bars 22, 24, 25 & 37). Nonetheless, the above reading is somewhat hypothetical, that is why it is not cited along with the main text.

Bars 31-32 R.H. In **FE** (→**EE**) there is no tie on the *d#²*.

Bar 32 R.H. The topmost note struck in the first chord is, in **A** (→**FC**) and the first editions, *b¹*. A comparison with the analogous bar 16 indicates Chopin's probable *lapsus calami*—an anticipation of the note to appear in the next chord (cf. *Ballades in G minor* Op. 23, bar 193 and *in F* Op. 38, bar 173). In **FES** Chopin altered the *b¹* to *a#¹*.

Bars 33-35 The pedal signs here have been placed by Chopin over the top stave, perhaps to underline the close connection between the pedaling and the sound of the long notes in the upper voice. A majority of later collected editions transfer the signs to their usual place under the bottom stave.

14. Prelude in E flat minor, Op. 28 no. 14

Sources and editorial principles
See *1-24. Preludes, Op. 28* on page 6.

p. 33   *Bar 1* In **FES** the description **Allegro** has been struck out and replaced with **Largo**. This could have been a lesson-time correction of a working nature—an indication of the method of practice and not a change in the concept of the *Prelude*. The placing of this *Prelude* described as **Largo** between *Preludes in F#*—**Lento** and *in Db*—**Sostenuto** seems improbable considering the construction of the entire cycle.
FE (→**EE**) wrongly gives the time signature as **c**.

Bar 5 In **A** (→**FE**, →**FC**→**GE**1) there are missing naturals before the ninth quaver to raise the *cb* to c. Chopin corrected himself by adding the accidentals in **FES**.

Bar 8 There is an illegible dynamic sign on the fourth beat which in **FC** (→**GE**) has been taken to read >= and in **FE** (→**EE**) =<.

Bar 14 Most of the later collected editions arbitrarily added flats in front of the eighth quaver of the bar raising the *ebb* to *eb*. Some editions also change the notation of the fourth and sixth quaver from *ebb* to d. Cf. similar adulterations in the finale of the *Sonata in Bb minor* Op. 35, bars 35-37.

15. Prelude in D flat major, Op. 28 no. 15

Sources and editorial principles
See *1-24. Preludes, Op. 28* on page 6.

p. 34   *Bars 3, 7, 22 & 78* L.H. Stems lengthening the sound of the *ab* on the second and sixth quaver of the bar can be found in **A** in bar 3 (both) and bar 7 (the first). It certainly could not have been Chopin's intent to perform these details in different ways, and so we give a unified notation based on bar 3 which has been recorded the most precisely.

Bar 4 RH. The 7 notes closing the bar are given in **EE** as semiquavers. The seemingly incorrect notation of the original was most possibly meant by Chopin to suggest that the group is played calmly and slightly slower. Cf. bar 79 of the same *Prelude*, and also *Prelude in F minor* Op. 28 no. 18, bar 12, and *Nocturnes* Op. 9: *in Bb minor* no. 1, bar 73 and *in Eb* no. 2, bar 16.

Bar 12 L.H. On the third quaver in **A** (→**FC**→**GE**1, →**FE**) there is no b to lower the *c¹* to *cb¹*. Chopin added it in **FED** and **FES**.

Bar 17 L.H. The seventh quaver in **A** (→**FE**→**EE**) is just *f¹*. Probably an erroneous reading of **A** resulted in the second *eb¹-f¹* to appear in **FC** (→**GE**). In such instances, Chopin's manuscripts are difficult to decipher, nonetheless in **A** this place is fairly clear —and obviously differs from the second *eb¹-f¹* in bar 15.

Bar 19 L.H. The crotchet stem at *gb* is found in **A** (→**FC**) but has been omitted in the first editions. In **FES** and **FED** Chopin added stems to the *gb* and *ab* notes.

p. 35   *Bar 21-22* The =< sign has been added on in **FES**.

Bar 26 R.H. *p* was added by Chopin in **FED**.

Bar 33 & 49 L.H. The final crotchet in **A** (→**FC**→**GE**, →**FE**→**EE**) is an octave *C#-c#*. It is clear from **A** that Chopin most probably altered an earlier sixth *E-c#*. However, in all the pupils' copies which Chopin annotated—**FED**, **FEJ** and **FES**—the octave was changed back to a sixth. We assume *E-c#* to be the final version adopted by Chopin, perhaps after many trials.

Bars 34 & 50 The taking over of *e* by the R.H. was marked on **FES**.

Bars 43-44 **FE** (→**EE**) omits *p* in bar 43. In **FED** Chopin added *pp* on to the beginning of bar 44.

p. 36   *Bar 65* R.H. At the beginning of the bar in **A** (→**FC**→**GE**, →**FE**) ♯ is erroneously placed in front of the *d#¹*. The mistake was corrected in **FES**.

p. 37   *Bar 68* R.H. **GE** is missing the *d#¹* in the first chord.

Bar 70 R.H. The main text is derived from **A** (→**FC**→**GE**1). Chopin is not likely to have made a mistake in **A**, as proved by the following arguments:

— in **A** the lower note of the chord (*d#¹*) is written very clearly,
— the octave suspension *d#¹-d#²* in a natural way resolves to the sixth *e¹-c#²*,
— it is characteristic of Chopin to go from an octave to a bigger distance in his chords or figurations; cf. e. g. *Preludes in F# minor* no. 8, bar 6, *in E* no. 9, bar 2, *in C minor* no. 20, bar 2 & 6, and *in F* no. 23, bar 14.
The **FE** (→**EE**, also in **GE**2) version given in the variant is probably the result of a mistake made by **FE** engraver, but the absence of corrections in the pupils' copies indicates that Chopin allowed it.

Bars 75-76 R.H The slur given in parentheses was added in **FE**S.

Bar 79 The mark which suggests how the run should be divided vis-à-vis the L.H. is contained in **FE**D.

Bars 81-83 The moment of releasing the pedal taken at the beginning of bar 81 is not indicated in **A** (cf. *Performance Commentary*). In **FC** (→**GE**) there are no pedal signs for these bars. In **FE** (→**EE**) there is a star (possibly not authentic) to signify pedal release in bar 81.

16. Prelude in B flat minor, Op. 28 no. 16

Sources and editorial principles
See *1-24. Preludes, Op. 28* on page 6.

p. 38   *Bar 1* **FE** (→**EE**) erroneously gives the time signature as **c**.

Bar 2 RH In **GE**, the second and third semiquaver have been switched, so the beginning of the bar reads *f²-eb²-c²-db²*.

Bar 7 R.H There is no accidental to precede the thirteenth and fifteenth semiquaver in **A** (→**FC,FE**). There could be doubts over ♮ placed on the same level before the third semiquaver (*a²*), whether Chopin intended *a³* or *ab³*, however more arguments are in favour of two *ab³* notes:
— precisely speaking, the script in **A** represents for this version, as ♭ is not vital here;
— the absence of accidentals indicates that Chopin was hearing the same sound twice; *a³* as the fifteenth note in this melodic and harmonic context would have sounded awkward;
— in the analogous bar 23 there are two *ab³* notes.
EE contains the version which we have adopted (with ♭ preceding the thirteenth note of the bar), while in **GE** there is ♭ arbitrarily added in front of the fifteenth note of the bar, which suggests the progression *a³b³ab³g³* on the last beat.

p. 39   *Bars 12 & 13* R.H. Before the twelfth semiquaver in **A** (→**FC**,**FE**) ♮ is missing.

Bar 16 L.H. In **A** (→**FE**→**EE**), there is a three-note chord *a-c-gb¹* on the second quaver. In **FC** there is an illegible *c¹* (or there is no note at all), so that **GE** only gives the seventh *a-gb¹*.

Bar 17 L.H. **FC** (→**GE**) has an erroneous *eb* instead of *f* in the chord.

p. 40   *Bar 22 & 23* R.H. **FC** (→**GE**) is missing ♮ in front of the seventh semiquaver in bar 22 and the third one in bar 23.

Bar 23 R.H. Most of the later collected editions change the ninth semiquaver from *f³* to *fb³*.

Bar 24 L.H. In **GE** on the second quaver there is an erroneous octave *gb-gb¹*. In some later collected editions this appears as *gb-c¹-gb¹*.

17. Prelude in A flat major, Op. 28 no. 17

Sources and editorial principles
See *1-24. Preludes, Op. 28* on page 6.
We have tacitly replaced the obvious omissions of chromatic signs in **A**, which are more frequent in this *Prelude* than in the others (the omissions have been replaced to a greater or lesser degree in the remaining sources).

Additional sources:
AM   Autograph of a fragment (bars 65-72) written in an album belonging to Ignaz Moscheles, and dated "Paris, 9 November 1839" (British Library, London).
FCI   Fontana's copy (Gesellschaft der Musikfreunde, Vienna) made from a lost autograph of an earlier version of the *Prelude*.

p. 42   *Bar 5* L.H. The chords in the second half of the bar in the **GE** are missing *ab*.

Bar 11 R.H. In some of the later collected editions the octave *db¹-db²* on the fourth quaver features an additional and arbitrary *g¹* note.

Bar 19 R.H. **A** (→**FC**→**GE**, →**FE**→**EE**) is missing ♯ before the topmost note of the chord at the fifth quaver. This must be a mistake of Chopin's, since:
— there is ♯ before the note in **FC**I,
— the chord contains a L.H. *e¹*, which would give an unpleasant clash with *f¹* (cf. bar 21, where Chopin avoids a similar clash by omitting *g#¹*).
R.H. The last chord of **FC** (→**GE**) is missing a *d¹*.

p. 43   *Bars 37-42* In **FE**2 (→**EE**) pedaling has been added, most probably by Fontana, duplicating bars 5-10.

p. 44   *Bar 43* R.H. In **A** the arpeggio mark before the chord at the fourth quaver merged with ♯ before the grace-note *c#²*, to resemble a ♮. Hence both **FE** (→**EE**) and **FC** (→**GE**) omit the arpeggio, and also in **FE** (→**EE**) the second grace-note is *c²*. Chopin corrected **FE** errors in pupils' copies: in **FE**S he wrote ♯ in place of ♮, in **FE**D he wrote in the arpeggio.

Bars 44-45 and 48-49 R.H. Most of the later collected editions tied *b¹* in bars 44-45 and *c#²* in bars 48-49. There are no ties in **A** (→**FC**→**GE**, →**FE**→**EE**) but they are back in **FC**I, however this is no argument that Chopin forgot about them in **A**, since the copy hands down the original concept of the prelude, which differs from the final one in respect of the R.H. on-the-beat strokes in bars 19-50. This is borne out—along with the ties in the bars discussed—by the following details in **FC**I: the tied *g#¹* in bar 19, *c#²* in bars 20-21, *b¹* in bar 43 (without the ornament), a missing *f¹* at the beginning of bar 37 and the chord at the beginning of bar 47. That Chopin did not mistakenly omit the ties is also proved by all the three pupils' copies annotated by him (**FE**D, **FE**S, **FE**J), where none appear.

Bar 53 The dynamic sign *p* or *pp* was written by Chopin in **FE**D.

p. 45   *Bar 65* L.H. In **A** (→**FE**→**EE**) there is no *fz*. This must certainly be an omission of Chopin's—it is the last bar on the page in **A**. The sound is accented by *fz* in **FC**I as well as in **AM**, and there is the testimony by Chopin's pupil, Mme Dubois (see quotes *about the Preludes...* preceding the musical text). *fz* is also featured by **FC** (→**GE**).

Bar 69 In part of the later collected editions the chords from the third to the sixth quaver contain added notes *eb¹* and *db¹* analogously to bar 77.

Bars 86-87 R.H. In **EE** and most of the later collected editions the crotchets *ab¹* have been lengthened with dots—contrary to **A** (→**FC**→**GE**, →**FE**) and **FC**I.

18. Prelude in F minor, Op. 28 no. 18

Sources and editorial principles
See *1-24. Preludes, Op. 28* on page 6.

p. 46 *Bar 1* FE (→EE) erroneously gives ¢ as the time signature.

Bar 8 None of the sources has a chromatic sign before the penultimate note of the run (both hands). This is obviously an omission, as proved by similar melodic figures in bars 4-5 (b♭ at the beginning of bar 5) and an octave higher in the bar discussed (e♭). Cf. the notes to *Prelude in C minor* Op. 28 no. 20, bar 3.

Bars 8 & 12 In GE the runs in these bars are noted in demisemiquavers. Although in bar 12 this is formally grounded we preserve Chopin's notation in the belief that it was purposeful (the demisemiquavers could have unnecessarily suggested the need to accelerate movement considerably). Cf. commentary to *Prelude in D♭* Op. 28 no. 15, bar 4.

p. 47 *Bar 17* R.H. GE1 is missing *e♭¹* in the arpeggio passage.

19. Prelude in E flat major, Op. 28 no. 19

Sources and editorial principles
See *1-24. Preludes, Op. 28* on page 6.
The pedaling, which is inaccurate in several places in A, we correct after more precisely recorded, analogous fragments.

p. 48 *Bars 1 & 33* R.H. The third quaver in A (→FC→GE1, →FE→EE) is *e♭¹*. In GE2 this has been altered to *g¹*, perhaps in analogy to bar 9. It does seem, however, that the difference between bars 1 & 9 was intended by Chopin, probably because of the relation to the preceding harmony (in bars 8-9) or its absence (bars 1 & 33). Cf. similar differentiation between bars 1 and 9 in the *Etude in E♭*, Op. 10 no. 11.

Bars 9-12 & 41-42 In FE2 (→EE) pedaling has been added (one pedal on bars 9-12 and one on 41-42). This is most probably not authentic (and certainly wrong in bars 9-12).

Bar 12 L.H. In all sources the seventh quaver is *c*. However, there exist indications to suspect that Chopin wrote the note mistakenly instead of *e♭*:
— the parallel fifths between extreme voices *c-g²* and *c♭-g♭²* at the beginning of the next bar,
— the lack of pedaling in bars 9-12 which suggests that Chopin was hearing the same harmony as in bars 1-4,
— the possibility of Chopin's *lapsus calami*, by which he anticipated the note which was to appear in the following bar (cf. commentary to *Prelude in F#* Op. 28 no. 13, bar 32).
Nonetheless, the above statements do not push the balance decisively towards the composer's mistake:
— parallel fifths between extreme voices can indeed be found in sources (e. g. *Prelude in E minor* Op. 28 no. 4, bars 3-4, *Mazurka in B♭* Op. 17 no. 1, bars 14-16, *Scherzo in E* Op. 54, bars 55-56),
— several inaccurate and even erroneous pedal signs in this prelude in A suggest that Chopin could have written them down in haste.
That is why in the main text we give the *c* found in the sources.

p. 50 *Bar 49* L.H. The main text—eighth quaver *g*—is derived from A (→FC→GE1, →FE→EE). In the analogous bar 57 the corresponding note is *b♭*. In bars 49-66 Chopin changed the pitch of the central notes in the triplets twelve times in A, six times replacing *g* with *b♭* in the E♭-major chord. In this situation it is probable that the first bar of this section remained uncorrected by an oversight (it happened that Chopin missed a correction in several similar places—see e. g. the commentary to *Prelude in F# minor* Op. 28 no. 8, bar 17). That is why we include the version with *b♭* as a variant.

Bars 53 & 61 L.H. The seventh and ninth quaver in GE1 is erroneously E♭ and B♭.

p. 51 *Bar 69* In FC (→GE) as well as in FE (→EE) there is in mid-bar a star signifying pedal release (added by Fontana). It does not feature in A, which means that the pedal depressed in bar 68 should be held through to the end of the prelude. Both the sound effect (pedal held) and notation (no ❋) are typical for Chopin and appear at the close of many of his compositions.

20. Prelude in C minor, Op. 28 no. 20

Sources and editorial principles
See *1-24. Preludes, Op. 28* on page 6.

Additional sources:
AB Autograph presented to Alfred de Beauchesne, dated "Paris, 30 January 1840" (Bibliothèque Nationale, Paris). It contains a first version of the work which does not have bars 9-12.
ACh Autograph contained in an album of Anna Cheremeteff, dated "Paris, 20 May 1845" (Russian State Library, Moscow).
CGS Copy made by George Sand, possibly from another, lost autograph (private collection, photocopy in: K. Kobylańska, *Rękopisy utworów Chopina*, Cracow 1977).

p. 51 *Bar 3* R.H. Before the top note of the final chord in A (→FC→GE, →FE) and also in AB there is no ♭, thus it should be read *e¹*. However, Chopin wrote ♭ in ACh and FES, and there is also *e♭¹* in CGS. It is thus all the more probable that the difference does not signify doubts or a change of concept on the part of Chopin in respect of this detail, but that it is an omission. Similar omissions of accidentals, which restore the pitch appropriate to the key are Chopin's most frequent errors—see notes to bars 8 & 12 of this *Prelude*, and also to *Preludes in A* op. 28 no. 7, bar 13, and *in F minor* Op. 28 no. 18, bar 8.

Bars 5 & 9 L.H. In ACh the slur starts on the second crotchet.

Bars 8 & 12 The description *ritenuto* appears in A (→FC) over bar 8 (the word begins over the end of bar 7). Since bars 9-12 are marked in abbreviated fashion as a repetition of bars 5-8, *ritenuto* should also be applied in bar 12, although FE (→EE) does not record this. The process of shaping the final version of the prelude could lead to a further interpretation of A being adopted, with *ritenuto* only applied in bar 12; as from Chopin's annotation on A (see the quotes *about the Preludes...* preceding the musical text) it arises that bars 9-12 were added on as a result of somebody's suggestion to a piece he considered already finished. Probably in A Chopin was copying bars 1-8 from an earlier, 9-bar version of the prelude, with a slowing of tempo towards the end of the composition, and he missed the need to shift *ritenuto*. From the aesthetic point of view, slowing tempo only in bar 8 or twice in a composition this short seems unfounded.
In AB and ACh the description is missing. In GE it appears only in bars 11-12.

Bar 8 (12) R.H. In AB the *g* notes in the final two chords are tied. This autograph does not have bars 9-12 thus it is not clear whether in the full version of the work the tie should figure in bar 8, or 12, or in both.

Bars 8 & 12 R.H. In A (→FC,FE) there is ♮ missing before the semiquaver to restore *d¹*. Chopin added the sign in FES, it also appears in AB and ACh.

Bar 12 ***f*** was added by Chopin in FED.

Bar 13 ***ff*** appears in AB.

21. Prelude in B flat major, Op. 28 no. 21

Sources and editorial principles
See *1-24. Preludes, Op. 28* on page 6.

p. 52

Bar 4 In **A** the minim g^1 was initially to continue through the entire bar. The prolonging dot was then deleted by Chopin, probably because of the eb^1 to be played by the R.H. on the last quaver of the bar (this is confirmed by the fingering marked on **FE**S and **FE**J). The lack of a rest to complement the R.H.'s rhythm may have provoked the erroneous notation of **FC** (→**GE**), where this eb^1, played on the fifth quaver of the bar, closes the R.H. phrase as a crotchet.

Bar 6 L.H. Sources give the fourth quaver without ♮ before the top note.

Bar 23 R.H. We give the version from **A** (→**FC**, →**FE**→**EE**) which does not arouse any doubts. **GE**1 is missing ab^2 in the grace-note and first crotchet. **GE**2 replaces grace-note cb^2-cb^3 with db^2-db^3. Some of the later collected editions have arbitrarily adopted the version from bar 31.

Bars 23 & 31 R.H. **A** (→**FC**→**GE**1, →**FE**) is missing ♭ lowering a^2 to ab^2.

p. 53

Bar 41 R.H. In some of the later collected editions the sixth gb^2-eb^3 has an arbitrarily added a^2.

Bars 45 & 47 L.H. In **FE**S the 3 final quavers of bar 47 have an added upwards beam. This probably means that they are taken over by the R.H., which we also note in the analogous bar 45.

p. 54

Bar 50 L.H. **GE** gives an erroneous octave A_1-A on the third beat.

Bars 50-52 R.H. In **GE**2 the minims g-g^1 in bars 50 and 52, and also f-bb-f^1 in bar 51 have been arbitrarily prolonged with dots.

Bar 54 In **FC** (→**GE**) this bar, which is similar to the previous one, is missing ("haplography")—cf. notes to bars 78-79 of *Prelude in G# minor* Op. 28 no. 12.

Bar 55 In **GE**1 the fourth quaver is erroneously given as Bb.

22. Prelude in G minor, Op. 28 no. 22

Sources and editorial principles
See *1-24. Preludes, Op. 28* on page 6.

p. 54

Bar 1 **FC** (→**GE**1) has no ties on a and c^1. In **GE**2 there is only a tie on c^1.

Bars 1-12 & 34-38 L.H. The slurring in analogous phrases in **A** is inconsistent. There are differences both in the length of the slurs and in the places where they begin and end. Much of this can be explained by difficulties with space (caused by the texture itself or by crossings), and by adding the slurs at different times, sometimes hurriedly. It is not possible to ascertain Chopin's notation in a manner which would not arouse doubt, that is why we recreate the version from **A**, together with certain suggestions on its interpretation featured in the *Performance Commentary*.

Bar 8 R.H. In **A** (→**FC**→**GE**) the bar numbers seven quavers: |♪ ♪♪ ♪|. Thus arises the question, what was the rhythmical value intended by Chopin for the chord: crotchet or quaver? As the three initial elements of the bar (♪, chord, ♪) figure quite accurately over the three initial L.H. quavers, this is the more probable value. This is also the interpretation adopted in **FE** (→**EE**).

p. 55

Bars 22 & 30 In the manuscripts, bars 17-24 have been subtitled with letters which are then used as abbreviated references to denote bars 25-32 which are repetitions. In bar 22 (and 30) the letter "f" is erroneously printed in **GE**1 as the dynamic sign *f*. In some of the later collected editions, this faulty marking shifted to bars 23 and 31.

Bars 35-38 R.H. In **A** (→**FC**→**GE**1, →**FE**1) the inner notes of the chords are not tied. This does not seem to be Chopin's omission—it would have concerned as many as five ties, while the striking of entire chords here reflects the growing dynamic and emotional force of the fragment. The ties have been added in **FE**2 (→**EE**) and **GE**2. Since Chopin's participation in Fontana's proof-reading of **FE**2 cannot be excluded, we give this version in a footnote.

Last bar Both the notation and the method of execution (cf. *Performance Commentary*) of the final chord arouse doubts. We give the notation after **A**; in **FE** (→**EE**) the lower slur is missing, the grace-note appears as a small crotchet and the RH chord is preceded by the wavy line of the arpeggio. **FC** (→**GE**) has the following notation:

23. Prelude in F major, Op. 28 no. 23

Sources and editorial principles
See *1-24. Preludes, Op. 28* on page 6.

p. 56

Bar 13 L.H. The second quaver is hardly legible in **FC**, that is why **GE** incorrectly took it for the second f^1-g^1.

Bar 14 R.H. In some of the later collected editions the sixth and fourteenth semiquaver has been arbitrarily altered from g^2 to b^2.

p. 57

Bars 15 & 16 L.H. We follow the notation of **A**. In remaining sources the record of rhythmical values is garbled.

Bar 16 L.H. **FC** (→**GE**1) is missing the f^2 note.

Bar 21 L.H. **GE**2 arbitrarily alters the eb^2 to c^2. **GE**3 restores the eb^2.

24. Prelude in D minor, Op. 28 no. 24

Sources and editorial principles
See *1-24. Preludes, Op. 28* on page 6.

p. 57

Bars 5 & 23 R.H. **GE** gives an erroneous a^1 at the end of bar 5 and e^1 at the end of bar 23.

p. 58

Bar 17 R.H. In **FC** (→**GE**) f^3 is erroneously given as a crotchet.

p. 59

Bar 31 L.H. **FC** (→**GE**) has an incorrect D as the second semiquaver in both figures.

Bar 42 L.H. **FE** has an incorrect cb on the second semiquaver in both figures, and **EE**—eb. **GE** gives an erroneous eb as the third semiquaver in the second half of the bar; some of the later collected editions also changed gb into eb in the first half of the bar.

p. 60

Bar 51 The dynamic sign in **A** is unclear: in **FC** (→**GE**) it has been read as *f* and in **FE** (→**EE**)—*ff*. Considering the subsequent *cresc.* and *ff*, we adopt *f*.

25. Prelude in C sharp minor, Op. 45

Sources
[A1], [A2]—lost autographs on which the first French and German editions were based (see quotes *about the Preludes...* preceding the musical text). Comparing these versions one can conclude with strong probability that the earlier manuscript [A1], completed with slightly less care, was used for the French edition. In later years it became an unvarying habit with Chopin to send the earliest of two or three manuscripts to the French publishers.

FE1 First, three-page French edition by M. Schlesinger (no publication number), Paris, 12 December 1841. The *Prelude* was part of the anthology *Keepsake des Pianistes* containing works by 12 composers. **FE**1 is based on [A1] and—considering the large number of errors it has—it was not proof-read by Chopin.

FE2 Second, seven-page French edition (same company, M.S. 3518), imprinted not long after the first. It recreates—in some places inaccurately—the text of **FE**1 and revises it, mainly as regards accidentals (over 50 replaced signs). However, the edition not only failed to correct the most glaring mistakes (e. g. in bars 43, 56 and 58) but added new ones (bars 18, 43, 48). It is impossible that Chopin proof-read the edition.

FE3 Later impression of **FE**2 by G. Brandus et S. Dufour, Paris, after 1858. Musical text and publishing number is unchanged.

FE = **FE**1, **FE**2 and **FE**3.

FEJ copy of **FE**2 from a collection which belonged to Chopin's sister, Ludwika Jędrzejewicz (Chopin Society, Warsaw), containing several corrections of printing errors made by Chopin's hand.

GE First German edition, Pietro Mechetti qᵐ Carlo (P.M.Nº 3594), Vienna, November 1841, based on [A2]. The edition was part of the album *Beethoven*, which featured 10 works by different composers. It is possible that Chopin proof-read the edition. There are copies which have different details on the cover.

EE First English edition by Wessel & Stapleton (W & S No. 5297), London, January 1842, based on **FE**1. Chopin had no part in it.

Editorial principles:
The basis is **GE**, in comparison to **FE**.

The pedal markings are not consistent between **GE** and **FE**. In those places, where the two seem to suggest a different execution we submit both versions; for easier notation and reading, **FE** pedaling is given without parentheses. We retouch some places, where the editions most probably misread the manuscripts.

p. 62 *Bar 1* Part of the later collected editions altered the time signature from ¢ to c.

Bar 2 R.H. **GE** is missing the grace-note b^1. This seems to be an omission made by the engraver, since the slightly bigger space between two crotchets can signify that a grace-note had been intended between them, but was forgotten in the engraving process. Cf. *Etude in F minor* Op. 10 no. 9, bar 64.

Bars 6-7 & 87-88 We feature one symbol ⟩ for both these pairs of bars, as it is in most other analogous places. The notation in **FE**1 as well as **GE** is inaccurate: in bars 6-7 **FE**1 and **GE** in 87-88 have new symbols for each bar (possibly because of starting a new line), and **GE** does not have the symbol in bar 6.

Bar 8 & analog. R.H. In **GE** and **FE** the first octave in the second half of the bar is generally given erroneously as 𝅘𝅥𝅭 or 𝅘𝅥𝅭 . This must have been the result of a misunderstanding. We lengthen the sixth or seventh quaver, although this is not con-sistently noted in the sources: **FE** (→**EE**), in bar 8; **GE** in 8, 22, 50 & 87. We believe there is no doubt that the "harmonic legato" (sustaining the components of harmony with fingers) should be applied in all similar figures.

Bar 9 R.H. **FE** (→**EE**) is missing a grace-note at the beginning of the bar.

Bar 9 & analog. R.H. The arpeggio can only be found in **GE** in bar 9. It would seem that Chopin thought it obvious in the further part of the prelude, that is why we give it in brackets in all analogous places. Arpeggio with a repetition of the bottom note is one of the most typical Chopin ornaments.

Bar 18 L.H. In **FE**1 there are no chromatic signs in this bar (also in the RH). This incomplete version was incorrectly adjusted in **FE**2 by adding ♯ before the first quaver. **GE** and **EE** have d (with naturals) throughout the bar. A relevant handwritten correction also appears in **FE**J. The ♮ before the penultimate quaver (G) is only found in **GE**.

Bars 18-19 R.H. The tie on a appears only in **GE**. In some of the later collected editions not only the a is sustained but also—arbitrarily—$f\#^1$ and a^1.

Bar 22 L.H. In **FE** (→**EE**) there is $g\#^1$ and a^1 erroneously on the third and fourth quaver. **FE**J contains a handwritten correction of this.

Bars 22 & 26 R.H. In the second half of the bar **FE** (→**EE**) omits to mark the prolongation of the first and third quaver.

p. 63 *Bars 31-32* *f* in bar 32 is found in **GE** and in bar 31—in **FE** (→**EE**). Since there are no manuscripts one cannot exclude the possibility that the difference resulted simply from an incorrect reading by engravers. We give priority to the **FE** version which we believe is more probable.

Bars 33-35 The only dynamic marking in these bars in **FE** (→**EE**) is ⟨ in bar 34.

Bar 36 **GE** features *p* here, possibly incorrect, as there is already a *p* in bar 35. That is why we adopt *pp* after **FE** (→**EE**).

p. 64 *Bar 43* R.H. In **FE**1 the second crotchet is erroneously c^2-ab^2-cb^3, "corrected" in **FE**2 to cb^2-ab^2-cb^3. In **GE** and **EE** the error does not appear.

Bar 48 R.H. **FE** (→**EE**) has the rhythm 𝅘𝅥𝅭 𝅘𝅥𝅮 in the top voice. Most probably this version is not correct (possibly the rhythm originally also figured in bars 36, 40 and 44 in [A1] and Chopin changed it; in the discussed bar this correction could have been missed or inaccurately introduced—the latter could be supported by **FE**1 where the final c^3 is placed after g^2, contrary to the rhythmic values).

Bar 49 R.H. **GE** is missing a^2 in the chord. We adopt the **FE** (→**EE**) version, as compared to the analogous bar 41. Also the obvious omission of a note in bar 54 in **GE** indicates it was highly possible that a part of the chord could have been overlooked here.

Bar 51 R.H. The arpeggio appears in **FE** (→**EE**).

Bar 52 L.H. In some of the later collected editions the final note has been altered from a^1 to $f\#^1$.

Bar 54 **GE** does not have $g\#^1$ in the chord, an obvious mistake.

p. 65 *Bar 56* L.H. **FE** incorrectly gives B_1 as the first note.

Bar 58 R.H. In the first chord **FE** (→**EE**) erroneously gives db^1 and db^2 instead of d^1 and d^2. Chopin corrected this in **FE**J.

Bars 62-63 The slurring of the main text is derived from **GE**, and that in the footnote—from **FE** (→**EE**).

Bars 67 & 71 R.H. The main text recreates **GE** and the variants—**FE** (→**EE**). Chopin could have wavered between these versions:

— ♩. ♪ reflects the motifs as they previously appeared,

— ♩ ♩ prepares the rhythm of bar 75 and in a way announces the transition to the end passage.

p. 66 *Bars 77-78* In **FE** (→**EE**) *ritenuto* figures in the second half of bar 77.

Bar 78 𝆑 appears only in **GE**.

Bar 79 Most of the later collected editions arbitrarily added the bar-line before the *Cadenza*.

Cadenza In **FE** (→**EE**) it has been printed using notes of a normal size and without the annotation *a piacere*. Cf. similar instances of erroneous reading of manuscripts in the *Mazurka in C*, Op. 24 no. 2, bars 70-88 or the *Scherzo in B♭ minor*, Op. 31, bars 281-284.
FE2 is missing the description *dimin*.

Bars 90-91 **GE** is missing the slur over the chords.

Jan Ekier
Paweł Kamiński